ARCTIC WORKHORSE

St. Roch *on her trials in English Bay, Vancouver.*
(Vancouver Maritime Museum, Gillen Collection)

ARCTIC WORKHORSE

The RCMP Schooner *St. Roch*

James P. Delgado

TouchWood
EDITIONS

TouchWood Editions Ltd.
Victoria, B.C., Canada.
This book is distributed by The Heritage Group, #108-17665 66A Avenue, Surrey, B.C., Canada, V3S 2A7.

Cover design by Pat McCallum; book design and layout by Retta Moorman.
Front-cover image courtesy of Commonwealth Insurance Company and Tom Parks; back-cover photograph of *St. Roch* frozen into the ice courtesy of *St. Roch* NHS, and of a crewmember unloading cargo at Cambridge Bay courtesy of the Vancouver Maritime Museum.
Maps by Eric Leinberger, from the Vancouver Maritime Museum collection.
This book is set in Goudy.

TouchWood Editions acknowledges the financial support for its publishing program from The Canada Council for the Arts, the Government of Canada through the Book Publishing Industry Development Program (BPIDP) and the Province of British Columbia through the British Columbia Arts Council.

Printed and bound in Canada by Transcontinental Printing.

National Library of Canada Cataloguing in Publication Data

Delgado, James P., 1958-
     Arctic workhorse: the RCMP schooner St. Roch / James P. Delgado
Rev. ed.
     Previous ed. has title: Dauntless St. Roch.
     Includes bibliographical references and index.
     ISBN 0-920663-86-9

     1. St. Roch (Schooner) 2. Northwest Passage. 3. Royal Canadian
Mounted Police—History. I. Delgado, James P. Dauntless St. Roch. II. Title.

FC3963.D45 2002   910'.9163'27   C2002-911297-4
F1090.5.D45 2002

The Canada Council | Le Conseil des Arts
for the Arts | du Canada

BRITISH
COLUMBIA
ARTS COUNCIL
Supported by the Province of British Columbia

CONTENTS

Acknowledgments — vi

Dedication and Donors — vii

Introduction — ix

CHAPTER ONE: The Quest for the Northwest Passage — 1

    Sidebar: The Arctic — 8

CHAPTER TWO: Policing the Arctic — 9

    Sidebar: *Maud* — 14

CHAPTER THREE: *St. Roch* Before the War, 1928-1939 — 15

    Sidebar: Life on Patrol — 22

    Sidebar: Henry Larsen — 28

CHAPTER FOUR: Through the Northwest Passage — 30

    Sidebar: Navigating in the Arctic — 36

CHAPTER FIVE: Back Home Again — 39

CHAPTER SIX: Preserving a Legacy — 45

CHAPTER SEVEN: Anatomy of a Ship — 53

    Sidebar: Characteristics of *St. Roch* — 58

    Drawings of *St. Roch*: Profiles, Plans and Section — 59

Appendix One: Chronology of St. Roch's Voyages — 64

Appendix Two: Members of the Crew — 64

Appendix Three: Members of the Crew of St. Roch II Voyage of Rediscovery — 67

Glossary — 68

Bibliography — 69

Index — 70

ACKNOWLEDGMENTS

This is a revised edition of *Dauntless St. Roch*, which was published in 1992 on the 50th anniversary of the ship's first voyage through the Northwest Passage. In 1992, several friends and colleagues made that book possible. Leonard McCann, Curator Emeritus of the Vancouver Maritime Museum, opened his voluminous research files on *St. Roch*. The research files of the Canadian National Parks Service, which operated *St. Roch* National Historic Site (NHS), were also made available through the support of Site Manager Gordon DeJean. Particularly helpful was former *St. Roch* interpreter Nancy Oliver, whose detailed, extensively researched resource guide for the ship is a wealth of material and an important piece of scholarship. In 1992, Ann West, Marlyn Horsdal, Leonard McCann and Gordon DeJean read the manuscript and offered many suggestions.

The 2002 edition also benefited from the editorial eye of Tara Knight and Ann Goodhart. Production assistance from Tara Knight and Betty Marshall helped speed along the second edition of this now-retitled work.

Most of the photographs in this book are from the collections of the Vancouver Maritime Museum; the others are from the collections of *St. Roch* National Historic Site. Among the photographs in both collections are images provided by former *St. Roch* crewmembers, including Bill White, Joe Olsen, John Duke and Captain Kae Boggild. The cover photograph was provided by Image Network Inc./Andrew Klaver & Russ Heinl, Courtesy of Commonwealth Insurance Company.

Any errors and omissions are the sole responsibility of the author.

DEDICATION

This is for the volunteers of the Vancouver Maritime Museum, who make the museum and the ship come alive and care for the treasures in the collections, and for the donors, sponsors, supporters and the dedicated crew of the *St. Roch II* Voyage of Rediscovery and the *St. Roch* Preservation Campaign, who kept the dream going.

DONOR BOARD
St. Roch II Voyage of Rediscovery
July 2000 – December 2000

Partners
Alcan
Canadian Heritage
MAN Engines
Millennium Bureau of Canada
RCMP
The Globe and Mail
TrendWest Resorts
TwinDisc/Arneson

Sponsors
Galleon's Lap Photo
TeeKay Shipping
Vancouver Foundation

Sponsors: In Kind
Ford of Canada
Infosat Telecommunications
Ken Kirkby
Kobelt

Kongsberg Simrad
Northern Transportation Co.
OceanVision Systems
RDI Marine
Vancouver School Board
Weston

Suppliers and Supporters
2XFudge
Allen Cadenhead
Allied Shipbuilders
AquaMarine
Arctic Operations International
BC Marine Trades Association
Benwell Atkins
Canada Place
Canadian Hydrographic Service
Datastar Marine
Douglas & McIntyre
Dry Zone

Dunbar Lumber
E-Cubed
Fiddler Productions
Focus Communications
Ice Sports
International Longshore
   Workers Union
International Paint
Lionel Johnston
Mako Marine
Mounted Police Foundation
Mustang Survival
Nauticomp
Nobeltec

Ocean Cement
Pacific Marine Training, BCIT
Port of Prince Rupert
Port of Vancouver
Robert Allan Ltd.
Rogers Video
Rolla
The Communications Group
The Portables
Universal Maritime Consultants
Yamaha
ZF Marine
Zodiac Hurricane

DONORS TO THE *St. Roch* PRESERVATION CAMPAIGN

The Vancouver Maritime Museum thanks the following generous supporters of *St. Roch*. (Donations to *Isumataq*, a dramatic Arctic landscape painted by Canadian artist Ken Kirkby, contributed to the *St. Roch* Preservation Campaign, helping build *St. Roch*'s endowment fund inch by inch. *Isumataq* contributors are identified by an asterisk.)

$100,000 +
Alcan
Millennium Bureau of Canada
TrendWest Resorts

$50,000 +
MAN Engines
TwinDisc/Arneson
TeeKay Shipping

Department of Canadian Heritage
Vancouver Foundation

$25,000 +
Fiddler Productions

$10,000 +
Mounted Police Foundation

$5,000 +
Commonwealth Insurance Company
Institute of Chartered Shipbrokers
    (B.C.)
James P. Delgado
Melusine Foundation
St. Lawrence Starch Company
    Limited
Tilbury Cement
Yamaha Motors Canada

$1,000 +
Cecilia Addy
Aventis Behring Canada Inc.
Bithel Holdings Ltd.
Ian Bruce Campbell
Dr. Wallace Chung*
Cloverdale Dist. 4 RCMP*
Douglas & McIntyre
Judy Hunt (for Pat Hunt)*
Jackman Foundation*
D.R. Lukin Johnston
Kaatza Foundation
Kiwanis Club of Evergreen
Chris McCallister
Mt. Newton Lodge
Neptune Bulk Terminal (Canada)
    Ltd.*
Dieter Riedel (for Henry Larsen)*
Robert Allen Ltd.
Jim Stoddart
Teleflex (Canada) Ltd.*

$500 +
Margot Allingham
Earl De Armond
Ruth Chudley
Robert Cuthbert*
Margaret Dymond
Thomas Forrest

Institute of Chartered Ship Brokers,
    B.C.
R.J. Kierzek
Edward Knight
Sandra McCormick
Mollie McDonald
George McLaren
Maurice Nadon
Marcus Nairn
RCMP Veterans Association,
    Vancouver
RCMP Veterans Ladies Auxiliary
Mary Rooney
Lisa Smith
Peter Stanley
Sylvia Stard
Margo Wood

$200 +
Helen & Philip Akrigg*
Robert Baragan
B. Bonnington
Botham Holdings Ltd.*
Peter Burns
Duncan Bury
Canadian Labour Views Co. Ltd.
Mary Carr
Charlotte M. Cliff-Talbot*
E. Alan Clutchey
Columbia Plastics
Michael Craddock
Coral Davis-Fry
Commodore Jan Drent
Larry Dunlop*
Dennis Farrell
Lawrence Greenwood
Dave Gordon*
Robert Halliday*
Ronald Hall
Doug Hatelid*

Eleanor Heslop
David Holmes
Ernest Howard
Bridget Jensen (for Derek Parkes)*
David Johns
E. & L. Kardos*
Roger Kembel
Maureen & George Kermack
Frances Kolotyluk*
Dr. Ken Kolotyluk*
William MacDonald
Dean McDonald
Kenneth & Audrey MacGowan
Peter McRae
Joy Mancinelli
Marion Magee
James Miller
Edward Neumiller
Marjorie Olds
Dr. Gerald Philipson
Hale Ramsey
Doreen & Dieter Riedel
Stephanie Robb*
Keith Sanderson
Robert Sanderson
Nick Shaigec
Roy Silverthorn
O.J. Sims
Richard Small
Peggy Smith*
David Stratton
Sunshine Coast Power and Sail
    Squadron
Garry Torp
Richard and Francis Walpole*
Gwen Walwyn*
Jan Van Weel
Wirtanen Electric Ltd.
Nancy Woodward

Continuing Supporters
Robert Baragan
B. Bonnington
Peter Burns
Canadian Labour Views Co. Ltd.
Mary Carr
Ruth Chudley
E. Alan Clutchey
Columbia Plastics
Commonwealth Insurance Company
Michael Craddock
Coral Davis-Fry
James P. Delgado
Commodore Jan Drent
Dennis Farrell
Thomas Forrest
Ronald Hall
D.R. Lukin Johnston
R.J. Kierzek
Marion Magee
Kenneth & Audrey MacGowan
George McLaren
Marcus Nairn
Edward Neumiller
Dr. Gerald Philipson
Doreen & Dieter Riedel
Keith Sanderson
Robert Sanderson
O.J. Sims
Lisa Smith
Sylvia Stard
St. Lawrence Starch Company
    Limited
David Stratton
Sunshine Coast Power and Sail
    Squadron
Jan Van Weel
Nancy Woodward

Introduction

The most famous Canadian vessel in Arctic exploration is preserved ashore in Vancouver, at the Vancouver Maritime Museum. The Royal Canadian Mounted Police (RCMP) auxiliary schooner *St. Roch* is internationally significant — she was the first vessel to sail through the Northwest Passage from west to east and only the second to sail through the passage from east to west. She was also the first ship to circumnavigate North America. *St. Roch's* long service in the Arctic as a floating detachment and supply ship of the RCMP has given her an important place in Canadian history. The RCMP were, to all intent, the only extension of the government in the north, a region with rich resources and a unique culture — a prize claimed by several nations. *St. Roch* helped to firmly establish Canadian sovereignty in the north through her presence and through her epic Northwest Passage voyages of 1940-1942 and 1944.

The City of Vancouver and a group of history-minded citizens moved *St. Roch* ashore in 1958 to preserve and restore her. Now administered by the Vancouver Maritime Museum, *St. Roch* was previously operated by Parks Canada, who meticulously restored the ship to her 1944 appearance. The ship is crowded with provisions — tins of biscuits, canned goods, sacks of coal, barrels of fuel and oil. The spartan, cramped cabins and forecastle are decorated with family photographs, uniforms hanging from hooks, a book or a magazine left on the bunk. The radio broadcasts the news and music of the period, and the calendar on the engine-room bulkhead notes that the date is September 4, 1944.

A tour through *St. Roch* is like stepping back in time. The crew has gone ashore and only the visitors remain on board. The intimate touches that evoke the crew are matched by the sense of inherent danger — the massive timbers in the hold that protect the hull from being crushed in the ice, the spare rudder lashed to the bulwark and the thick steel shoe at the bow to split the ice floes. *St. Roch* is special not just for her history, but for the experience she offers. The ship is a unique artifact of Arctic endurance, a compelling symbol of human endeavour in a forbidding land and of ordinary men rendered extraordinary by unusual and extreme circumstances at the top of the world.

James P. Delgado
Vancouver, B.C.
2003

Chapter One

THE QUEST FOR THE NORTHWEST PASSAGE

The quest for the Northwest Passage, an oceanic shortcut from Europe to the Pacific across the top of the world, is one of the greatest stories in the annals of exploration and discovery. Following Columbus's encounter with the Americas, the search for a route through the continent, instead of the long and arduous voyage by way of the tip of South America, dominated the attention of Spain, Britain and other European powers for three centuries. By the 19th century, the quest for the Northwest Passage was a major initiative of the British Admiralty because the preceding 250 years of exploration had shown that the passage could only lie in British-claimed territory, in the Arctic north of Canada.

The search for the passage, its eventual discovery and the intervening saga of human endeavour in the far north are filled with tales of struggle, sacrifice and perseverance. Less than a century after Columbus's first voyage, an English expedition led by Martin Frobisher sailed to the shores of Baffin Bay to reach what Frobisher believed to be the water passage through the Americas to Asia. However, Frobisher's voyages of 1576, 1577 and 1578 failed to find such a passage. He was

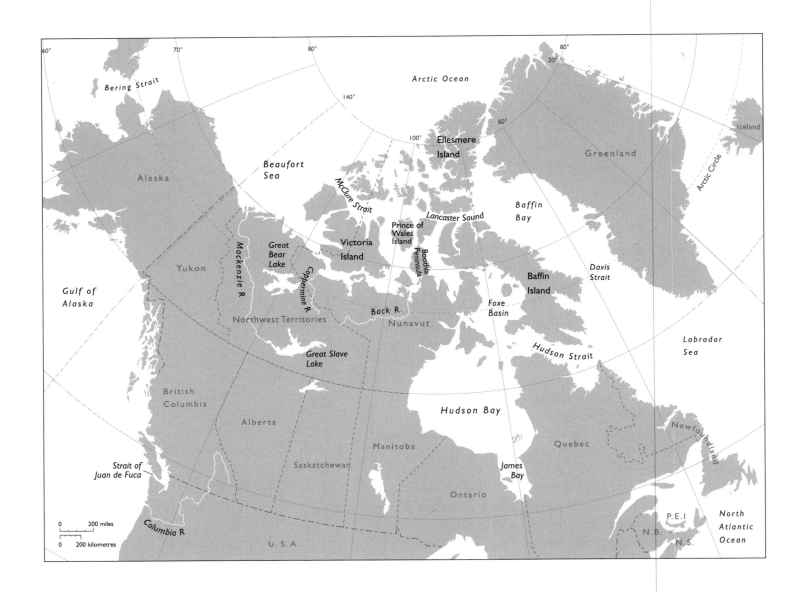

in a dead end, literally and figuratively, as his water route to Asia proved to be a long bay, now named after him.

In the wake of Frobisher, subsequent maritime expeditions pushed farther north: in 1585 John Davis probed the eastern shores of Baffin Island; in 1616 Robert Bylot and William Baffin, aboard the barque *Discovery*, sailed to the northern end of Baffin Bay and reconnoitred Lancaster Sound, which much later would prove to be the actual entrance to the Northwest Passage. Then another false passage diverted the attention of other explorers, who charted the vast reaches of Hudson Bay, hoping it was the elusive strait. Henry Hudson was the first. He penetrated Hudson Strait in 1610 and entered the bay that now bears his name before mutineers cast him adrift and left him to die. The Hudson's Bay Company, chartered in 1670 to exploit the rich fur resources of the bay and its surrounding territory, was little interested in the passage, but its vessels ultimately did conclude the search on the bay with the 1762 discovery that what had seemed the most promising opening, at Chesterfield Inlet, ended instead in the mouth of a small, shallow river.

Conjecture that an entrance into the passage existed on the northwest coast of America sent Spanish and British explorers to the Pacific to find it. James Cook visited the coast of what is now British Columbia in 1778 but did not find evidence of a passage. Between 1792 and 1795, one of Cook's junior officers, now Captain George Vancouver, made a return voyage to search the same coast for evidence of a passage. Instead, he put to rest the notion of a western entrance to the passage. In 1794, while anchored in Nootka Sound on the coast of what is today Vancouver Island, Vancouver wrote that he had "truly determined the non-existence of any water communication between this and the opposite side of America within the bounds of our investigation beyond all doubt and disputation..." Vancouver was correct; to reach the western end of the passage, he would have had to sail north, through the Bering Strait and past Point Barrow to reach the Beaufort Sea.

Meanwhile, overland expeditions probed the Arctic. Samuel Hearne and Matonabbee, his Chipewyan guide, traced the Coppermine River to its mouth between 1770 and 1772. Alexander Mackenzie, a fur trader with the North West Company, pushed north from Great Slave Lake, following the river that now bears his name, in 1789. Thanks to these explorers, the vast, icy seas of the Arctic had been sighted, and expeditions followed to explore by both land and sea. A Royal Navy expedition led by Lieutenant John Franklin marched north to chart the coast near the mouth of the Coppermine River between 1819 and 1822. John Ross, in command of the ships *Isabella* and *Alexander*, retraced Bylot and Baffin's voyage in Baffin Bay in 1818. Lieutenant William Edward Parry, in HMS *Hecla* and *Griper*, sailed immediately after Ross's return and pushed into Lancaster Sound — and hence the passage itself, in 1819. Before he was finally stopped by the onset of winter and the ice, Parry also sailed through the passage, penetrating farther into the Arctic than his predecessors. His successful survival at "Winter Harbor" showed that it was possible to be frozen in and survive in that icy wilderness.

Both Parry and Franklin returned to the Arctic in 1824-1825. The admiralty sent Captain William F. Beechey, RN, in command of HMS *Blossom*, into the Pacific to attempt to round Alaska, enter the Arctic and press east to reach Parry and Franklin. The three expeditions failed to make contact, but mapped more of the passage. A gap in the middle of the Arctic, a blank spot on the map, showed where the probable "last link" in the Northwest Passage was. Finding it, or "forging the last link," would take decades and cost Britain several ships and hundreds of men.

Parry's Hecla *enters the Northwest Passage, 1819.* (VANCOUVER MARITIME MUSEUM)

Building an igloo, from Parry's second voyage in search of the Northwest Passage. (VANCOUVER MARITIME MUSEUM)

Parry's luck ran out on his third expedition when his ship *Fury*, pushed ashore by ice, had to be abandoned and two crews crowded into Parry's flagship, HMS *Hecla*, to escape the Arctic. John Ross, whose 1818 voyage mapped Baffin Bay, returned to the Arctic in 1829 on a privately funded expedition to seek the passage. Sailing past where Parry had lost *Fury*, Ross disappeared for nearly four years, pushing into Prince Regent Inlet and then south into the dead end of the Gulf of Boothia. Trapped in the ice for three winters, Ross abandoned his ship *Victory* and marched with his surviving men to Fury Beach. There, supplies landed from Parry's wrecked ship sheltered and fed them for another winter. In 1833, out of food and fearing another, fatal winter, Ross and his men barely escaped with their lives in small boats that they sailed and rowed to the mouth of Lancaster Sound.

Land-based expeditions, including one to find Ross, while not successful in locating the lost explorer, did add a great deal to the knowledge of the region. Naval officer George Back and Hudson's Bay Company officers Peter Dease, Thomas Simpson and John Rae charted the coast in the vicinity of the Boothia Peninsula and Victoria Island in the 1830s and 1840s, and after two decades of exploration and struggle filled in much detail on the charts, narrowing the gap of unknown lands and seas to a small area.

The most disastrous Arctic expedition finally provided the impetus for completing the task of exploring and charting the Northwest Passage. In 1845, Franklin, now a 59-year-old member of the peerage, returned to the Arctic with 129 men in two ships, *Erebus* and *Terror*. After one winter at tiny Beechey Island, Franklin sailed south toward King William Island. Just off King William's northern shore, the ice trapped the two ships in September 1846. Nearly two years later, in April 1848, their crews abandoned them. Franklin was dead, as were several of his officers, whittled down by disease and the cold. The survivors attempted to march out to safety but never made it. Every man died. The greatest tragedy in the

Fury ashore and wrecked at Fury Beach, 1825.
(Vancouver Maritime Museum)

Sir John Franklin.
(VANCOUVER MARITIME MUSEUM)

history of Arctic exploration, the fate of Franklin and his men inspired a decades-long search, first for the survivors and then for the truth of what had happened.

The admiralty, Franklin's widow, Lady Jane, and the United States government sent out expeditions to find Franklin. In all, more than 32 separate attempts were made between 1849 and 1859. Hudson's Bay Company explorer John Rae recovered relics of Franklin's and in 1854 learned from the Inuit of the fate of the crews of the lost ships. Rae's findings, including tales from the Inuit that the last of Franklin's men had resorted to cannibalism, were controversial, so in 1857 Lady Jane Franklin hired Captain Francis Leopold M'Clintock to head north and seek other news of her husband's fate. Over the next two years M'Clintock traced Franklin's route, discovering relics and scattered skeletons and the only written note ever located, a brief account of how the ships had become trapped and then abandoned.

This imagined scene depicts Franklin's ships Erebus *and* Terror *wintering in the ice.*
(VANCOUVER MARITIME MUSEUM)

The expeditions searching for Franklin reached and charted the various channels and straits that comprised the Northwest Passage. The route to the Pacific was now known, but Britain, weary of the cost, abandoned the quest. It took a new century and the skill of a Norwegian navigator to see the Northwest Passage completed.

In 1903, Roald Amundsen equipped the 30-year-old fishing sloop *Gjøa* for the voyage through the passage. The 42-ton vessel was small and light, powered by sail and a 13-horsepower engine. It was a perfect choice for the shallow, ice-choked straits of the route. Sailing in June, Amundsen pressed into the Arctic, wintering off King William Island in a harbour he named "*Gjøahavn*," or Gjoa Haven. He stayed for over a year, taking scientific observations and making an over-the-ice trip in search of the magnetic North Pole. In August 1905, *Gjøa* left her snug harbour and wove her way through difficult channels to reach the Beaufort Sea in September. Trapped by ice there, *Gjøa* wintered off King Point.

In July 1906, Amundsen sailed past Point Barrow, through the Bering Strait and into the Pacific, ending his voyage in San Francisco where *Gjøa* was beached for permanent public display. The long quest was over — the Northwest Passage had been conquered at last.

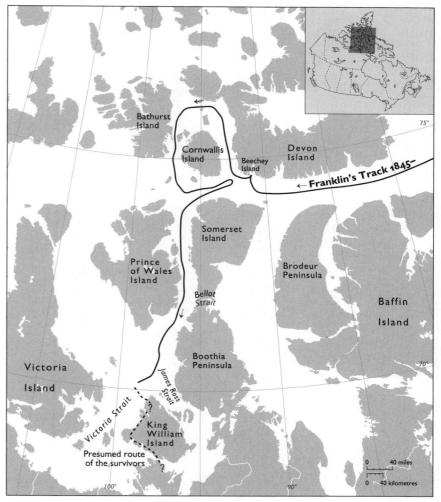

Gjoa at the end of her voyage through the Northwest Passage, 1906.
(VANCOUVER MARITIME MUSEUM)

THE ARCTIC

The Northern Temperate Zone, in which most of Canada, Britain, Russia and the Baltic countries are located, gives way to the Arctic at the Arctic Circle, an imaginary line drawn by geographers at the parallel of 66 degrees, 32 minutes north. North of this parallel is the top of the world.

To many, the Arctic is a cold, barren land where survival is difficult, if not nearly impossible. In fact, the eight million square miles of land in the Arctic include the taiga, or forested plains of spruce and fir and some hardwoods; the tundra, a flat expanse of moss, lichens and swamps that breed clouds of mosquitoes in the warmer months; and finally, far to the north, ice and snow. The ice, which covers some of the land and large portions of the four million square miles of the Arctic Ocean, advances and retreats with the seasons and in response to the global climate, so that some straits and passages may be open one year, and choked and blocked with ice the next.

The coldest temperature ever recorded in the Arctic was -90 degrees F. at Verkhoyansk in northeastern Siberia. The average temperature, however, is 30 degrees F., while in the summer temperatures can reach as high as 70 degrees F.

Author Farley Mowat divides the Canadian Arctic into six distinct geographical regions — the "Icy Mountains" of Baffin, Ellesmere and Devon islands; the "Canadian Sea" of Hudson Bay; the "Barren Lands" west of the bay that are the northern extension of Manitoba's and Saskatchewan's prairies; the "Northern Prairies" that include the Boothia Peninsula and King William and Victoria islands; the "Western Highlands," and the mountains of the Yukon that occupy the northwestern corner of Canada; and the "High Arctic" islands, remote and scarcely visited.

The Native people of the Arctic, once known as the Eskimo, are now referred to by their own name for themselves: Inuit. These former nomads survived in a subsistence culture, foraging in the sparse Arctic landscape. Outstanding hunters and navigators, the Inuit were better equipped for Arctic survival than the European explorers who "discovered" them. Canada claims most of the Arctic north of North America, and has asserted sovereignty over most of the islands that form the Arctic archipelago. The majority of Canada's population lives within 125 miles of the border with the United States, though the bulk of the landmass lies to the north of them. Even now, with ready access by air, and the development of oil-drilling and mining, much of the Arctic remains unknown and unvisited, a mysterious land for those whose national territory encompasses it.

Chapter Two

POLICING THE ARCTIC

The new national government of the Dominion of Canada, established in 1867, created the North West Mounted Police force in 1873. The NWMP functioned as a semi-military organization, enforcing law and order, and acting on behalf of the national government to assert the dominion's interests on the Canadian frontier. At first this assertion was on the North American plains; it was later extended to firm control over the Klondike goldfields of the Yukon, and finally over the vast expanse of the Arctic, a region long considered Canadian by Canadians, but subject to the interests and incursions of others.

The influx of foreign miners with their potential for lawlessness brought the North West Mounted Police to the Yukon in 1894, and after the Bonanza Creek gold discovery of August 1896 and the resultant rush of 1897-1898, the Mounted Police found themselves upholding the law, thwarting the nationalistic sentiments of some American miners and adapting themselves to harsh frontier conditions in an unforgiving climate. It was a time and a place that helped shape the popular concept of the "Mounties" as rugged frontier police who kept crime at bay and never rested in their pursuit of criminals despite the terrain, weather or hardship.

In the years after the Klondike gold rush, Canada took an active interest in its Arctic possessions. Most of the Arctic had been claimed by Britain, and Canadian sovereignty in the region came slowly. In 1870, Canada had acquired Rupert's Land from the Hudson's Bay Company, and ten years later the remaining British possessions in the north were ceded to the dominion. Yet Canada did little to claim, hold or protect its interests in the region. The Arctic was left to whalers, traders and missionaries.

By the end of the 19th century, the Canadian government's interest shifted from the Klondike to the major American whaling outpost on Herschel Island. The government viewed the whaling station, 90 miles inside the Canadian border, as a provocative threat to its claims of sovereignty in the Arctic. Missionary complaints that the whalers who wintered at Herschel were debauching the Inuit were another cause for concern. The experience of the Klondike had proved the necessity of upholding Canadian sovereignty, and the worth of the Mounted Police in doing so. In 1900, the government tentatively formulated plans to place a Mounted Police detachment at Herschel Island. However, it took the force three years to muster the resources and the men for the Arctic; the first Mounted Police patrol of the island and the region around it was made in August 1903.

Despite the inherent difficulties of supply and isolation, and the hardships of a barren, desolate land, the Mounties established a post on the island the same year. The orders for the two-man detachment included collecting customs fees and duties, maintaining law and order, and putting an end to the trading of liquor to the Inuit. The same year, the Mounted Police established another Arctic post, a six-man detachment at Fullerton on Hudson Bay. Over the next few years, the force, now renamed the Royal North West Mounted Police, established other posts in the eastern Arctic and on the northern shores of Hudson Bay.

In 1904, the government of Sir Wilfrid Laurier, as part of a national plan to assert Canadian sovereignty in the Arctic, diverted the

Canadian Polar Expedition, under the command of Joseph Elzear Bernier, from its intended three-year exploration of the maritime approaches to the North Pole. Instead, the government placed Bernier and his vessel, *Arctic*, under the command of Mounted Police Superintendent J.D. Moodie and sent them north to show the flag and serve as a base for patrols and treks throughout the region. The "Eastern Arctic Patrol" of the Mounted Police and Captain Bernier, in a series of voyages, left plaques and cairns proclaiming Canada's ownership of the Arctic archipelago before it was cancelled in 1911.

However, officers of the various Mounted Police detachments, many of them reached only once a year by chartered supply ships, continued to range through the territory on patrols. The Mountie on dog-sled patrol is a romantic and popular image in Canadian history; it was also perhaps the most important part of the police's role in the Arctic as they regularly visited remote settlements, delivered mail, checked on game animals and provided visible proof of Canada's ownership of and interest in the region. Special patrols, formed to search for lost explorers, traders and missionaries, investigate crimes, found new detachments or simply explore, were another significant element. Occasionally, the government hired private vessels to assist the police. In 1914, for example, the police chartered the schooner *Village Belle* for a special patrol to capture the killers of two explorers. With the vessel as a base, the police investigated the murders, established good relations with the Inuit they visited and charted and mapped a thousand-square-mile area.

Constable Albert Chartrand and his team in 1940. The dog-sled patrol is an enduring image of the Mounties' work in the north. (VANCOUVER MARITIME MUSEUM)

The Royal North West Mounted Police became the Royal Canadian Mounted Police (RCMP) in 1919. Their headquarters, formerly in Regina, moved to Ottawa and, in the words of historian William Morrison, they became "less a force of the prairie and the frontier" and more of a city and town police force. Nonetheless, in light of concern over protecting Canadian sovereignty on Ellesmere Island from Danish interests, the government ordered the RCMP to establish detachments there in 1920. A 1922 expedition did just that. Again using chartered vessels, the RCMP opened seven detachments in the eastern Arctic between 1920 and 1927. From these posts, patrols reached many of the remote spots in the Arctic between 1922 and 1932, all part of an effort by the government to set up post offices, customs posts and police units "at strategic and necessary points" connected by the patrols.

With this control, albeit stretched thinly between the few government outposts, Canada moved to better conduct its affairs in the north. Modern conveniences such as the airplane and radio were introduced in the late 1920s and in the same decade, the RCMP decided to build their own ship capable of travelling into and remaining in the Arctic. The vessel would connect the RCMP's Arctic Sub-District's four detachments on a 1,200-mile stretch of coast; it would become a travelling unit, while supplying posts that had previously been the domain of chartered vessels. Frozen into the ice during the winter, the ship would serve as the base for long patrols in the classic tradition of the force. In other months it would move throughout the region as an efficient and effective demonstration of sovereignty and as an extension of federal power in the north.

The RCMP vessel was the idea of Stuart Taylor Wood, Assistant Commissioner of the RCMP, when he served as the officer commanding the Herschel Island detachment between 1919 and

Workers caulking the hull planks at the stern of St. Roch *in 1928 at Burrard Dry Dock Company.* (VANCOUVER MARITIME MUSEUM)

1924. Wood's successor at Herschel, Inspector Thomas B. Caulkin, resurrected the idea of an RCMP ship for the Arctic, bringing it forward to Wood in 1925. With Wood's endorsement, the RCMP finally approved the ship in 1927. Vancouver naval architect Tom Halliday designed the ship, working with specifications provided by Charles Druguid of the Department of the Marine in Ottawa and drawing on Halliday's own experience with other Arctic vessels, including the former polar exploration ship *Maud*. The federal government contracted the schooner's construction to the Burrard Dry Dock Company of North Vancouver. While Burrard Dry Dock had built many notable vessels, *St. Roch* would ultimately be the most famous product of the shipyard.

However, it was her accomplishments, not her style, that won *St. Roch* fame. As Henry Larsen, the longest serving and best known of the schooner's skippers, later remarked, "The ship was not exactly a beauty, but she was solidly built." The plans were drafted in November 1927 and shortly thereafter the yard laid the schooner down as Hull Number 114 on their ways on the north shore of Burrard Inlet. Veteran Vancouver shipwright Arthur Moscrop, hired by Burrard Dry Dock as a subcontractor, supervised the work. As it neared completion, the RCMP named the ship *St. Roch* for the East Quebec Parish of St. Roch, the constituency of the Federal Minister of Justice, Ernest Lapointe. All was ready for the ship's launch.

MAUD

The design and construction of *St. Roch* owes much to a Norwegian-built Arctic exploration ship specially designed for explorer Roald Amundsen. *Maud*, built near what is today Oslo, Norway, was a smaller, improved version of an earlier polar exploration ship, *Fram*. *Fram*, under the command of explorer Fridjtof Nansen, drifted in the polar ice pack in an unsuccessful attempt to reach the North Pole in the 1890s. In 1917, Amundsen, building on his earlier success from his navigation of the Northwest Passage between 1903 and 1906, and reaching the South Pole in 1911, decided to try where Nansen and *Fram* had failed.

Maud never reached the North Pole. Four separate attempts met with failure, and in 1925, Amundsen finally abandoned his quest to drift to the pole. He was bankrupt, and creditors seized *Maud* and sold her at auction to satisfy Amundsen's debts. The Hudson's Bay Company (HBC) purchased the ship to supply their Arctic outposts. After refitting in Vancouver, and with a new pilothouse and a new name, *Baymaud*, the ship sailed for the eastern Arctic in June 1926. She never returned. After freezing in for the winter of 1926-1927, the crew moored the ship close to shore at the settlement of Cambridge Bay for use as a floating machine shop, warehouse and wireless station.

In 1931 the ship sank, either due to a leak in the propeller shaft or, as some locals insist, because she was deliberately scuttled. Some of the ship remained above the ice and water, and the HBC and locals stripped the masts, rigging and cabins from the hull. Today, only a small area of the wreck's starboard side rises above the water. The rest of the ship lies in seven metres of frigid water.

St. Roch is in many ways a copy of *Maud*. When Tom Halliday drew up the plans for *St. Roch*, he added a number of elements from Amundsen's old ship. Just a year earlier, in 1926, the HBC had hired Halliday to oversee *Maud*'s refit before she headed north. Halliday copied the ship's lines and several construction details while planning *St. Roch*. These included a round, egg-shaped hull, thick ironwood planks that formed an extra layer of "ice sheathing" on the hull, a large cabin aft, a single-screw diesel engine, a rudder that could be lifted up through a special well to avoid being snapped off by ice and thick beams to brace the hold against the crushing pressure of ice floes.

Chapter Three

ST. ROCH BEFORE THE WAR, 1928-1939

Burrard Dry Dock launched *St. Roch* on May 7, 1928, at high tide. Gladys Newson, the wife of the officer commanding the Vancouver detachment of the RCMP, smashed a bottle of champagne against the bow as *St. Roch* began to slide down the ways and into the water. On May 10, 1928, the RCMP hired Captain William Hugh Gillen, an experienced Arctic hand and a former whaling and sealing captain, to serve as the master of the new schooner. Gillen's contract required him to navigate *St. Roch* to Herschel Island "as soon as ice conditions permit," for the sum of $1,000. If kept on staff after reaching the Arctic, Gillen would receive $200 a month "and keep." Constable Henry Asbjorn Larsen, a recent RCMP recruit but a 14-year veteran of the sea (including two years in the Arctic) was appointed mate. After fitting out and trials, the RCMP accepted the schooner on June 19, 1928. On her trials, held in English Bay, *St. Roch* developed a maximum speed of eight knots, which was considered sufficient. Sturdiness and just getting there were important; speed was not.

On Sunday, June 24, 1928, the Vancouver *Daily Province* reported: "MOUNTED POLICE CRAFT WILL SAIL ON TUESDAY FOR NORTHERN PATROL. Leading the way into the Arctic this season,

St. Roch just after being launched into the waters of Burrard Inlet. She is riding high because the machinery and masts have yet to be installed.
(VANCOUVER MARITIME MUSEUM)

insofar as the Vancouver northern fleet is concerned, the Royal Canadian Mounted Police patrol auxiliary schooner *St. Roch* will sail ... from the Evans, Coleman and Evans docks with a crew of R.C.M.P. constables and a civilian master ...."

The *Daily Province* reporter was impressed with the thick hull and described *St. Roch* as "fully equipped and modern in every respect." Despite the newspaper's assertion that "all the R.C.M.P. men on the vessel are experienced ice men and know Arctic conditions thoroughly," original crewmember Jack Foster later stated that only two of the ten men had been north prior to the voyage. Whether or not they were the only Arctic veterans, Gillen, Larsen and Joe Olsen were certainly the only seamen. Larsen, for one, claimed to be grateful for the fact. "I, for my part, was glad that we had not hired professional sailors, because I was sure that such men never would have worked out on a ship like this one. I am sure that the cramped bunks, the spartan food, and the ship as a whole would never have received the approval of real sailors. Our policemen were quite different, they were used to taking orders, and above all, they were all imbued with an esprit de corps and were particularly proud of the fact that they had been picked for Arctic duty, which always carried some extra prestige in the RCMP."

After a frenzy of loading the schooner with the 150 tons of cargo (including 30 tons of coal stowed in the hold) that *St. Roch* would carry north, the schooner sailed from Vancouver at 2:00 P.M. on the afternoon of June 26, 1928, just in time to catch the high tide. The voyage was uneventful as *St. Roch* cleared the harbour and entered the Pacific for the thousand-mile run north and west along

Gathered on deck, before the maiden voyage: (Front, L to R) T.G. Parsloe, J.J. Olsen, Captain Gillen, ?, ?; (Back, L to R) M.F. Foster, ?, Henry Larsen, W.J. Parry, ?.
(VANCOUVER MARITIME MUSEUM, OLSEN COLLECTION)

St. Roch *being prepared for her maiden trip to the Arctic. She is now riding lower in the water.* (VANCOUVER MARITIME MUSEUM)

the coast of Alaska and the Aleutians to reach the Bering Strait. The crew was miserable, though. The ship leaked, pitched and heaved on the open ocean, and most of the men were seasick. To make matters worse, on the second day out the engine was stopped and the sails were set, for, as Jack Foster explained, "She was supposed to sail most of the time." To the chagrin of Captain Gillen, *St. Roch* "just seemed to lean forward, buried her nose and refused to answer the helm." The blunt, ice-breaking bow did not cut through the water. "We often used canvas afterward," said Foster, "but only to help her along or to help stop rolling, which was one thing she could do quite well."

When *St. Roch* arrived at Dutch Harbor, the principal American outpost in the Aleutians, the Mounties topped off their fuel tanks and were entertained that evening aboard an Arctic veteran, the 16-year-old U.S. Coast Guard cutter *Unalga* (WPG-53). The American sailors visited *St. Roch* and, as crewmember Joe Olsen explained, they "certainly wondered about us when they ... saw riding boots and spurs and all the accoutrements of a cavalryman, and of course our men were properly dressed when in port, wearing the red serge and Stetson hat of the Mounted Police."

Passing through the Bering Strait, *St. Roch* was stopped by ice at Point Barrow. Gillen managed to work his way through it, though,

Constables Parsloe and Larsen holystoning (scrubbing) the deck with large sandstone blocks. (VANCOUVER MARITIME MUSEUM)

When St. Roch *stopped at Point Barrow in 1928, she was visited by some of the local Inuit and the settlement's teacher.* (VANCOUVER MARITIME MUSEUM)

and the schooner arrived at the RCMP detachment on Herschel Island on July 24, five weeks after sailing from Vancouver. With Gillen still in command, *St. Roch* sailed to Baillie Island and then to the RCMP detachment at Cambridge Bay on Victoria Island, dropping off supplies and transferring men before returning to Herschel. On August 28, as preparations were made to take *St. Roch* to Langton Bay, 370 miles east of Herschel Island, Captain Gillen and engineer Pat Kelly, an employee of the Union Diesel company who had come along to test

Constable Henry Larsen holding an Inuit child on Baillie Island, 1929; Inspector Vernon Kemp is behind Larsen. (ST. ROCH NHS)

Corporal Wall and Constable Fielder in front of the detachment at Baillie Island, 1928. (VANCOUVER MARITIME MUSEUM, TUDOR COLLECTION)

his firm's engine in Arctic conditions, said their goodbyes. In Gillen's place, Henry Larsen, technically outranked by his fellow constables but a seasoned Arctic veteran, would serve as master of the vessel, while Sergeant Andy Anderton commanded the police detachment aboard *St. Roch*.

Crewmembers readying the ship for the winter, constructing the frame-
work for the tent that will cover the deck.
(VANCOUVER MARITIME MUSEUM)

Constables Parsloe, Larsen and Kells with a load of fresh-water
ice for the ship's water supply, in Langton Bay, 1928.
(ST. ROCH NHS)

Gillen had done a fine job as delivery skipper for the schooner, and before he left he signed his official report on the performance of *St. Roch* on her first trip north. Gillen called her "a very satisfactory vessel," and seaworthy, but complained that "she rolls quickly" because of the round-bottomed hull. The ship handled well in ice, but the steering gear, in Gillen's opinion, was too heavy, and the rigging too light for Arctic service. However, the worst complaint was that "the decks leak badly, in fact when we first bumped into a heavy head sea after leaving Dixon Entrance on the B.C. Coast, with the spray coming over, every berth in the forecastle was wet from water leaking through the deck and skylight. Both the forward and after skylights have leaked ever since leaving Vancouver, the poop-deck over the cabin, galley, engine room and wireless room is leaking seriously for a new ship." Gillen praised the Union diesel, however. "The main engine is all that could be desired. I think I can safely say it has given better service than any other engine I have ever used."

When they arrived at Langton Bay, a 70-mile-an-hour gale blew *St. Roch* ashore. Larsen and the crew lightened the ship of most of her cargo and managed to get her free. They anchored the schooner, only to be blown ashore again in another storm. Larsen worried about being frozen in, hard ashore in the shallows, but managed to get *St. Roch* free of the beach and into deeper water. As the ice froze around the hull, locking the ship in for the winter, the crew stowed the sails and rigging and built a lumber-and-canvas covering for the deck. On the ice, the men worked to cut 40 tons of blocks that they would later melt for drinking water. They also erected an absolute necessity, a small igloo 25 yards from the ship known affectionately as the "ice palace," where nature's calls were heeded.

With the ship prepared for winter, the crew ceased being mariners and once again became active-duty policemen. The dogs, which had been picked up earlier, were hitched up to the sleds and drilled and exercised to get ready for the patrols that would take the crew far and wide over the Arctic. The first winter went well, and in June, as the

Constable Fred Farrar, clad only in his hat, takes a bath on laundry day while listening to the radio. (Vancouver Maritime Museum)

A group of Inuit on Herschel Island pose with Constable Albert Chartrand. (St. Roch NHS)

St. Roch *frozen in for the winter.*
(VANCOUVER MARITIME MUSEUM)

LIFE ON PATROL

Once the crew secured *St. Roch* for the winter, the Mounties prepared for their patrols. Most patrols were protracted affairs, many lasting two to three months. The dog sled was their only means of travel, with large 16- to 18-foot sleds used on the "trail." The Mounties thinly coated the steel runners of the sleds with mud, which, when smoothed and polished with bearskin and water and frozen, created a slick layer of ice. This allowed the sleds to be pulled "with a minimum of friction," as Larsen explained, because "steel pulls too hard over the frosty snow." Replacing the mud on the runners with oatmeal was a *St. Roch* innovation; if men were stuck on patrol without food, the oatmeal could always be thawed and eaten!

The sleds carried up to 1,500 pounds of supplies. "Of course there is not much riding as one constantly has to mind and watch the sleds." Nonetheless, with the sleds the constables could cover as much as 30 to 40 miles a day. At night, the dogs were unhitched from their leather harnesses, which were stowed away because the always-hungry animals would eat them, and tethered for the night after being fed dried fish and seal blubber. The patrolling Mounties would then build themselves an igloo or snow house before stripping and climbing into their caribou-skin sleeping bags.

The RCMP adopted Inuit clothing for patrols. Traditional parkas and pants were fashioned from hides of caribou, usually by Inuit who traded or sold them to the RCMP. Two suits of clothes were worn: the outer suit with the hair facing out, made from caribou killed in the winter when the hair was long and warm, and an inner suit with the hair facing in, against the body. The inner suits were fashioned from the hides of animals killed in the summer, when the hair was short and light. While warm, the suits had drawbacks; the inner layer tickled, and the outer layer shed hair, usually into the frying pan or tea pail.

As well as adopting Inuit clothing for their patrols in the Arctic, the RCMP built traditional Inuit houses. (VANCOUVER MARITIME MUSEUM)

Constables Larsen and Olsen, and Captain Gillen, posing on the ice in 1928. The RCMP wore traditional Inuit clothing when they were in the Arctic. (VANCOUVER MARITIME MUSEUM, OLSEN COLLECTION)

The crew cooked in advance the food that was carried on patrol. A special recipe of finely cut bacon, canned meat, tomatoes, onions, molasses, sugar, mustard and salt was boiled in a five-gallon pot until very thick. The crew ladled this mixture into pans and allowed it to freeze. Broken up by axe into small chunks that were packed into canvas bags, it was then ready for patrol. The Mounties also made patties of boiled rice, potatoes and vegetables with beef, boiled with canned soup and frozen for the trail. Instead of bread or hardtack, *St. Roch*'s crew fried hundreds of doughnuts.

Raw fish, cut into small slices and frozen, was also packed, and then eaten in this state; "This raw frozen fish gives one a warm feeling of well-being" and was an important staple. Flour and beef fat were brought on patrol for occasional bannock or pancakes. All this, with coffee and tea, was carried on the sleds and cooked each night over Swedish Primus stoves. Larsen and his Mounties swore by the Primus: "A finer implement for Arctic travelers, I think, has never been invented."

weather warmed and the ice began to thaw, the crew took down the winter housing, overhauled the machinery, painted the hull and made ready to sail. The ice cleared on July 9, 1929, and *St. Roch* sailed for Herschel Island on the 11th. Orders were waiting there to proceed back to Vancouver for repairs, and on August 26, *St. Roch* began the trip home. The maiden voyage ended a month later, on September 23.

In 1937, the ice pushed St. Roch *out of the water and crushed and sank the HBC ship* Fort James *while the two ships were anchored at Coronation Gulf. Crewmember Scott Alexander filmed the disaster.*
(VANCOUVER MARITIME MUSEUM, ALEXANDER COLLECTION)

St. Roch had logged 10,300 nautical miles. Larsen immediately set about having the ship repaired and her faults rectified at Burrard Dry Dock. He later recalled that his first voyage as master "had not been an easy trip for me. The responsibilities had been great, and even if the boys had been very helpful, they were anything but a well-drilled ship's crew as yet. The ship herself had presented many problems. She was new and untried .... But I guess this is the purpose of maiden voyages, to find out about these things."

During the next ten years, *St. Roch* returned to the Arctic for longer spells of duty. Between 1930 and 1934, she served in the Coronation Gulf area of the western Arctic, returning to Vancouver after four winters up north. It was the schooner's longest voyage. Resuming duties in the Arctic in 1935, she worked out of Cambridge Bay before arriving back in Vancouver in 1937. This was a difficult voyage, with heavy ice, hard winters and little game. It was also the voyage when *St. Roch*, caught in the ice with the Hudson's Bay Company ship *Fort James*, stood by helplessly as the HBC ship was crushed; *St. Roch* survived with rudder damage. Back in Cambridge Bay in 1938, the ship did not stay for long; with the outbreak of World War II, the RCMP recalled *St. Roch* in August 1939.

The 1930s had seen *St. Roch* and her crews fulfill every aspect of their duties as a patrol, transport and supply vessel for the RCMP. As crewmember Bill White, one of the original *St. Roch* hands, later explained, "At the time the RCMP was the Canadian government's only official presence in the north. There was no local government, no game wardens, no social workers, no military — the RCMP did it all." This meant that *St. Roch* had not only to supply the scattered RCMP detachments in the Arctic, but also to "carry mail, ferry Eskimo children to school, run sick people to the hospital, explore new shipping routes and perform all manner of official chores."

As a supply vessel, *St. Roch* brought the necessities of life to the isolated RCMP detachments she visited. In 1938, for example, the schooner left Vancouver with 132 tons of coal, 38 tons of fuel oil and gasoline, lumber and "various provisions and detachment supplies." Most of these supplies were unloaded by hand in the Arctic — long, tedious work with block and tackle, the men trying not to perspire too profusely in their Arctic gear since their sweat would freeze in the cold. As a transport, *St. Roch* carried Mounties in addition to her crew to and from the Arctic.

A crewmember breaks out cargo from the hold, using a boom slung from the mainmast, at Cambridge Bay.
(VANCOUVER MARITIME MUSEUM)

These men worked as members of the crew until they landed and on a few occasions, some of them stayed aboard as regular crew, trading places with another Mountie who then went ashore. *St. Roch* also carried

Inuit children bound for the residential school at Aklavik, as well as sick and injured patients headed to Aklavik's mission hospital.

St. Roch's radio, a relatively new technological innovation in the Arctic when the schooner arrived in 1928, proved invaluable. The Marconi 50-watt short-wave and 100-watt long-wave transmitters received much use, connecting the schooner with other Arctic radio stations and, via a network of receivers and transmitters, with the rest of Canada and headquarters. In 1937, the radio operator kept in contact with Coppermine twice a week, relaying the ship's messages as well as those of traders and trappers in the area.

When not occupied with other duties, the men went on hunting trips. As Henry Larsen later stated, "I went on some seal hunts and that helped, because even if our rations were ample, we also had to feed our company on our supplies. The RCMP has always been very strict when it came to rations." The introduction of fresh game also brought variety to the crew's diet. One crewmember, John Duke, wrote in a letter home, "We eat anything we can get a hold of that walks, swims or flies rather than the canned meat." Larsen, writing to his wife, explained that "anything fresh is scarce here no meat at all you know so I am constantly on the lookout for something or other with hair or feathers on it that can fly walk or crawl it all goes into the pot."

Occasionally, regular police duties were required, although Larsen would later remark, "Our police duties were the least of our problems." *St. Roch*'s crew had to investigate deaths and disappearances, and several patrols were raised when trappers, missionaries or traders were overdue. In all, *St. Roch*'s detachment investigated some 17 deaths — two suicides, mishaps by drowning and freezing, and a few murders, Larsen commenting later, "Other than the occasional murder, crime is almost non-existent among Eskimos."

In 1931, the crew arrested an Inuit woman who had shot and killed her husband. The courts acquitted the woman, ruling she had shot in self-defence. In 1932, an Inuk named Aqigiq, who had joined a wife-sharing arrangement with another man, killed his rival because the other man kept both women for himself. In another case, a man living with a couple killed his host when goaded into it by the wife. He confessed, but the corpse could not be found, and he was released. In 1936, a possible case of infanticide was investigated at Colburne. According to the official report filed by *St. Roch*'s crew, "As the child was a girl and the rumours which are current as to the natives killing off girl babies, it was considered advisable to enquire into this death but it was established to the satisfaction of everyone that it died a natural death."

St. Roch's crew also undertook several civic duties, including registering all vital statistics such as births, deaths and marriages. Another task saw them issuing numbered identification discs to the Inuit. "Eskimos were given numbers because they generally had one name and a lot of Eskimos had the same ones, and sometimes they even changed their name to something different. All this was very confusing in the records that people were trying to keep," according to one crewmember. The numbered tags were handed out by the various detachments, including *St. Roch*, and helped the Mounties to sort out who should get the government's Family Allowance, Old Age Pension and pensions for the blind. Since the RCMP was charged with the general welfare of the Inuit, Larsen and the crew of *St. Roch* were frequently called in to investigate social conditions, assist Inuit in relocating to better hunting or fishing grounds and stop any exploitation of the Inuit by the increasing number of white traders and trappers entering the region. The Mounties also collected fur-export taxes, sold game licenses, registered shotguns and rifles, paid a bounty on wolves killed by hunters when a pelt was presented and enforced game regulations.

The first 12 years of *St. Roch*'s career were an active, hardworking time in the Arctic, with their own unique adventures, challenges and tales. But they were largely forgotten by the public, who remember *St. Roch* more for her epic voyages through the Northwest Passage than for the years of devoted service in the north, unheralded except by those whose lives the schooner and her crew touched in the Arctic.

During the summer St. Roch *carried supplies between the various RCMP detachments and settlements. In this photograph she is anchored in Langton Bay in 1929.* (VANCOUVER MARITIME MUSEUM, TURNER COLLECTION)

HENRY LARSEN

Henry Asbjorn Larsen's lifelong passion was to follow in the footsteps of the great Arctic explorers. Born near the mouth of Oslo Fiord on September 30, 1899, at Frederikstad, Norway, Larsen grew up on the sea. His studies in geography and history gave him a hunger for "new lands and a curiosity for the history of the past." After an apprenticeship at sea that began at age 15, Larsen graduated from the Norwegian State Navigation School in Oslo, and served a six-month stretch of duty in the Norwegian navy. In 1922, he signed on as fourth mate of the steamer *Theodore Roosevelt*.

Theodore Roosevelt connected Norway with various Pacific coast ports. In Seattle, Larsen met the polar explorer Roald Amundsen and his pilot, Oscar Omdahl, who shipped back to Norway aboard Larsen's steamer. Larsen had his imagination fired by Omdahl's tales of the north, and despite a promotion to third mate, left *Theodore Roosevelt* in 1923 when the ship docked in Vancouver. In the spring of 1924, Larsen's chance to go north arrived when he sailed as the mate on the schooner *Maid of Orleans*.

Larsen's early experiences in the Arctic served him well later in life. In particular, he became friends with the RCMP constables living on Herschel Island. The policemen impressed Larsen, and he decided to join the RCMP, particularly if he could serve in the north. One of the Mounties, Inspector Thomas Caulkin, told Larsen that, in the opinion of a few of the RCMP's Arctic veterans, the

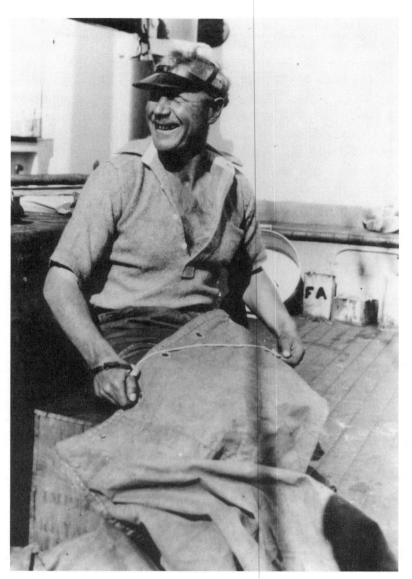

Henry Larsen grins as he patches sails.
(VANCOUVER MARITIME MUSEUM)

Henry Larsen in full dress order in his cabin, 1944.
(VANCOUVER MARITIME MUSEUM)

force would one day build and man a small schooner of its own for Arctic service. The thought appealed to Larsen. Returning with *Maid of Orleans* to Seattle, where he was paid off, Larsen made his way to British Columbia, working at odd jobs until the opportunity to join the RCMP arrived with the news of *St. Roch*'s construction.

Initially assigned as mate, Larsen assumed command of *St. Roch* in August 1928. In 1929, the RCMP promoted him to corporal. Following his first epic voyage through the Northwest Passage, in 1942, he was promoted to staff sergeant. Later made an inspector, Larsen, at the time of his retirement from the RCMP on February 7, 1961, was the officer commanding "G" Division, the Arctic. Henry Larsen received many honours during his career, including the Polar Medal, awarded to him and his crew in 1942 by King George VI, and the Royal Canadian Geographical Society's first Massey Medal.

Henry Larsen married Mary Hargreaves on February 7, 1935, in Vancouver, and they had three children — two daughters, Doreen and Beverly, and a son, Gordon. After Henry's retirement, he and Mary lived for a while in Lunenberg, Nova Scotia, but in September 1964 they moved to Vancouver, primarily to take charge of *St. Roch* as a museum ship. But Larsen was an ill man; he was admitted to hospital and died there, at age 65, on October 29, 1964. One of his last remarks, in a letter to a friend, was that he would "soon be setting out on that last, great sled patrol."

Chapter Four

THROUGH THE NORTHWEST PASSAGE

Tales of intrepid explorers had fired Henry Larsen's imagination when he was a boy in Norway, and had led him to sign on for an Arctic voyage with trapper and trader Christian Klengenberg in 1924. Larsen's desire to explore, and to navigate the Northwest Passage, was strong, and as captain of *St. Roch* he was in a perfect position. At first, the RCMP saw it differently. As early as 1928, Larsen told one of his superiors, "I'd very much like to put this ship through the Northwest Passage. She's built to take it and I believe she could do it." His comment was not acted on, and dreams of the Northwest Passage had to wait. In July 1936, Sir James MacBrien, the Commissioner of the RCMP, visited *St. Roch* on station at Cambridge Bay. Larsen pitched his idea again, but "I was told that our role was not to be explorers, but to carry out the various duties connected with the administration of the North .... But the Commissioner added that he also hoped that the opportunity to navigate from one side of the Arctic to the other would present itself one day."

The chance to attempt the passage came when Larsen and *St. Roch* returned from their fourth voyage and arrived in Vancouver in September 1939. Sent to Ottawa for a refresher course in police methods in early 1940, Larsen found himself in the office of Assistant

Commissioner Thomas Caulkin, who was then commanding "G" Division — the Arctic division — under Commissioner Stuart Wood. Caulkin had befriended Larsen on Herschel Island in 1926 and had influenced Larsen's decision to join the RCMP, particularly when Caulkin told him of the plan to build *St. Roch*. Together, the two friends went to see Commissioner Wood.

Wood and Caulkin, the two veterans of Herschel Island, had a plan for Larsen. "When Caulkin and I arrived in the Commissioner's office I was completely taken aback when I learned that I was to take the *St. Roch* into the western Arctic with a full load of supplies for ourselves, so that I could take the ship into the eastern Arctic in an attempt to reach Halifax .... In short we were assigned the task of sailing from the west to the east; if successful ours would be the first ship to conquer the Northwest Passage in that direction." Just as significant was the fact that *St. Roch* would also be the first ship to navigate the passage since Roald Amundsen had done so in *Gjøa* 35 years before. "So here it was," Larsen later recalled, "my great moment. Canada was at war and the government had realized the need to demonstrate the country's sovereignty over the Arctic islands."

The original impetus for the ship's Northwest Passage voyage was not to demonstrate sovereignty, however. At the request of Alcan, Canada's primary manufacturer of aluminum, the Canadian government was contemplating an occupation of nearby Greenland. Greenland, home to the world's largest cryolite mine (a critical ingredient in aluminum) was vulnerable to seizure by the Nazis as a colony of Nazi-occupied Denmark. *St. Roch* was one of the few vessels the government could spare for the "invasion" of Greenland, although by the time Larsen sailed, the government had called off the Greenland operation. The United States government had guaranteed the protection of the cryolite mines and Canada, hard-pressed in its naval war against German U-boats, had acquiesced. The cancellation of the voyage to Greenland notwithstanding, *St. Roch*'s orders to navigate the Northwest Passage remained in effect.

Constable Peters paints the triatic stay near the foremast at Yarrows; behind him is the naval dockyard at Esquimalt.
(VANCOUVER MARITIME MUSEUM)

Henry Larsen was equal to the task. He was Canada's most experienced Arctic navigator, a scholar of the sagas of Arctic exploration, and a man admired by the Inuit, to whom he was "Hanorie Umiarjuag, " or "Henry with the Big Ship," and whose help he would need to survive. With Wood's blessing, *St. Roch* put into the naval base at Esquimalt, near Victoria, for repairs to make her ready for the passage. Wartime exigencies meant that Larsen could not get the new, more powerful engine he wanted, but the bow was resheathed in steel, and a new auxiliary engine was added to charge batteries. *St. Roch* was completed in June 1940, and in Larsen's opinion, "She was in much better shape than she ever had been."

Larsen selected the southern route through the Northwest Passage: "Eastward through Queen Maud Gulf, south of King William Island, then northward between Boothia Peninsula and the King William Island Coast; or, in other words, we used the same route as taken by Amundsen in the *Gjøa* ... with the exception that we passed through Bellot Strait instead of Peel Sound."

St. Roch, the intent of her voyage a wartime secret, sailed from Vancouver in the early morning hours of June 23, 1940. Bad weather on the northwest run across the Pacific roughed up the crew, but on July 4, *St. Roch* cleared Unimak Pass and entered the Bering Sea. After a brief stop in Dutch Harbor, the schooner headed north, reaching Point Barrow on July 23. It was a bad year for ice, and Larsen had a difficult time dodging ice floes before he passed Barrow and pushed on to Herschel Island. From Herschel, *St. Roch* continued east to Cambridge Bay, her usual wintering spot. Larsen had hoped to proceed farther east and winter in Gjoa Haven, but "it was too late in the season." Thick ice and the danger of being frozen in and trapped in a bad spot sent *St. Roch* westward in retreat before the ice caught up with her at Walker Bay in September. It was there, on the west coast of Victoria Island, 300 feet from shore, that *St. Roch* wintered while Larsen plotted a new course north of the island, through Prince of Wales Strait and into Melville Sound. The schooner would not complete the Northwest Passage in 1940.

St. Roch broke out of her winter mooring on the morning of July 31, 1941. Instead of going east, however, the schooner was sent back to a longstanding port of call, Tuktoyaktuk, or "Tuk." Wartime shortages of transportation and the traditional duties of the RCMP called. Larsen and *St. Roch* had to wait another year before renewing the quest for the Northwest Passage. The delay also turned Larsen's attention back to the southern route through the passage — Amundsen's — when he discovered that the summer of 1941 had not cleared the ice sufficiently from his intended northern route. Throughout early August, *St. Roch* carried freight from Tuk to Cambridge Bay and Coppermine.

Sailing from Cambridge Bay on August 19, *St. Roch* now headed east once again, slowly working through the ice toward King William Island. On August 27, she dropped anchor in Gjoa Haven. Larsen decided to push on; within four days he was in sight of the Boothia Peninsula and close to where Franklin's ill-fated expedition had come to its deadly conclusion nearly a century before. The same waters were almost fatal for *St. Roch*. Racing against the advancing ice, Larsen stubbornly decided not to return to Gjoa Haven and surrender the hard-won miles he had wrested from the Arctic. The ice threatened to push *St. Roch* ashore, so Larsen headed for the only safe anchorage he knew of: Pasley Bay. Halfway up the west coast of the Boothia Peninsula, it was marked on an 1855 Admiralty chart. Larsen sailed for it.

Anchoring in Pasley Bay on September 3, Larsen landed on the peninsula and hiked up a nearby hill. From its summit he saw an unwelcome sight. The ice had closed in, trapping *St. Roch*. Back on board, Larsen was slowly forced down the bay, his engines overpowered by the massive force of the ice as it advanced. An opening in the ice brought temporary relief, but when Larsen anchored in a patch of open water, the wind shifted and *St. Roch* was pinned between heavy floes, a "helpless hulk" in Larsen's words, drifting with the ice.

When St. Roch *was under way, the crow's-nests or "ice buckets" atop the masts were manned by crewmembers watching for leads. Here two men — one clinging to the foremast — help the ship navigate through the ice.* (ST. ROCH NHS)

It was then that the ship was nearly lost. *St. Roch* hit a shoal and grounded; for another, more lightly built ship, it would have been disaster, as the ice ran over the stranded vessel. *St. Roch* pivoted twice, the ice throwing her to port and then to starboard. Ice pushed up over the starboard side, and chunks began to fall on deck. "I wondered if we had come this far to be crushed like a nut on a shoal and then buried by the ice," Larsen later wrote. The schooner was nearly on her beam ends, dragging her anchors and 90 fathoms (540 feet) of chain, when she slid free.

Larsen managed to hook a wire rope to a rock in the bay, and with 1,600 pounds of steel anchors paid out all the way and still dragging, he used the immovable outcrop as a natural anchor. Nearly ashore, *St. Roch* was quickly trapped when the wind died, the ice stopped flowing and the water around the ship froze. Working hard, the crew chopped the ship free and pushed her 50 yards farther offshore. It was there that *St. Roch* spent the winter.

It was a winter of hard, long patrols. Larsen and an Inuit guide, Equalla, reconnoitred the Boothia Peninsula on a 21-day, 320-mile patrol in December. Constable Albert Chartrand and Equalla made a longer, 28-day, 489-mile patrol to King William Island in January 1942. Tragedy struck on Chartrand's return. The popular constable suffered a fatal heart attack in the forecastle on February 13, dying almost instantly. "There was nothing anyone of us could have done to help him, and we were completely stunned," wrote Larsen. It was the only death suffered by *St. Roch*'s crew in the line of duty.

Shortly after Chartrand's death, Larsen, Equalla and Constable Pat Hunt made the longest patrol of the voyage, in part to contact a Catholic priest, Father Gustav Henri, who lived 400 miles away, so that he could travel to the ship in the spring and conduct a funeral for Chartrand. The 1,140-mile trek lasted from February through May. Larsen and Hunt reached Gjoa Haven by dog sled before turning back, and returned to the ship after a 71-day absence on May 6. Two weeks later, Father Henri arrived, and a requiem mass was held for

Chartrand. The constable was buried on a nearby hill, and the priest blessed the grave. Before they sailed, Chartrand's shipmates marked the site with a 15-foot-high rock cairn that remains there to this day.

On August 3, facing the real possibility that the ship would remain stuck for another winter, Larsen weighed anchor, pushed out of Pasley Bay and moved north. Caught by the ice once again, her stern out of the water and the bow nearly shoved under a floe, *St. Roch* was in danger. "I thought the end had come," wrote Larsen, but he used explosive charges to blast the floes, "which upended and formed a kind of cushion." Whenever possible, Larsen then pushed on, ramming the ice and following narrow leads. "Thus, little by little, the *St. Roch* made headway." On August 12, the Number 1 cylinder head in the engine cracked. The engineers blocked off the cylinder and with partial power — at a time when the schooner needed everything she had, and perhaps more — *St. Roch* continued up the coast of the Boothia Peninsula to Bellot Strait. It was a slow passage — she made 60 miles in 25 days.

The ship reached the entrance to Bellot Strait on August 29. "We had almost reached the point where we were going to congratulate each other on our good fortune," wrote Larsen. Instead, there inside the 18-mile-long passage *St. Roch* was once again almost lost. Ice racing into the strait jammed up against an ice floe that had stuck on a submerged reef. Larsen ordered full speed ahead and rammed *St. Roch* up against loose floating ice near one end of the floe. "There must have been thousands of tons of broken ice pressing up against the stranded floe." The schooner, wedged tightly, began to groan as her timbers strained. "Huge cakes of ice spun and gyrated in huge whirlpools. In some of the whirlpools we could see narwhals, lost and bewildered, with their long spiraled horns waving in the air as they stood almost upright in the water." For nearly an hour *St. Roch* was caught. Then the ice broke free, and they drifted through the waterway, coming to anchor at the Hudson's Bay Company's post at Fort Ross, at the eastern end of the strait.

A crewmember drops the eight-pound lead into the sea to test the depth of the water. The lead line was used constantly during voyages in the Arctic. (ST. ROCH NHS)

NAVIGATING IN THE ARCTIC

The greatest source of danger faced by *St. Roch* was the ice. Thick, always moving and inexorable in its massive force, the ice made sounds as *St. Roch* made her way through pack ice off Alaska that reminded crewmember Bill White of roaring dinosaurs and the creation of the world . In order to thread through the constantly shifting channels in the ice pack, Larsen kept a lookout "for the slightest change or opening, so that we could take advantage of it while we crept slowly eastward." For the most part, the job was Larsen's. He later wrote, "During the countless long hours I spent in the crow's-nest, I got the feeling that I had constantly to match wits with the moving pack ice. Many a time did I head for an opening in the ice only to watch it crash together just ahead of me, as if it were a living thing deliberately trying to keep me from reaching open water. On other occasions the ice would snap shut behind me, as if it held me in a trap. But it also happened that when things looked hopeless and I was almost resigned to giving up, the ice would suddenly open up as if by some magical force, and as the bell rang full speed ahead the leads would gradually get wider and wider and allow us to slide through the cracks for mile after mile."

Larsen pushed *St. Roch* in and out of the ice, probing up one channel for several miles, backing off, and trying another; "poking back and forth like a fly on the window," as Bill White described it. Larsen watched the ice floes, sometimes refusing to enter one "that looked wide enough to take the *Roch* sideways," according to White who, with the rest of the men wondered why, until the floe snapped shut "like a vise." At times, when the ice needed widening, Larsen ordered full speed ahead and rammed the floe with the steel-sheathed bow to crack it open. The skipper was particularly pleased in 1940, at the start of his first transit of the Northwest Passage, to get new, sharper steel sheathing: "With the almost knife-sharp bow we would be able to split even fairly heavy ice-floes."

On other occasions, particularly when *St. Roch* was wedged in the ice, Larsen resorted to blasting to free himself. "The charges were made up of about five pounds of black powder in a bottle, made watertight with Sunlight soap. We then inserted a fuse in the top and tied the bottle to a long pole." Larsen would climb out onto the ice with the

St. Roch *on her first trip north, in 1928, working her way through the ice to Herschel Island.* (VANCOUVER MARITIME MUSEUM)

pole, looking for an opening large enough to shove the charge down so that "it would explode a few feet below the ice. The sudden heave of the water then would lift the ice and crack it. It was imperative that the fuse be only a few inches long because the current often moved the charge or ice out of position and there was a danger that the charge could be carried under the ship and explode there. Once the pole came rushing back up through the hole where I had pushed it down. By our count it was almost ready to explode next to where Scott and I were standing. There was nothing else for me to do but grab the pole and push it down as far as I could and keep it down until it exploded. I was showered with water and small chunks of ice, and it gave me an uncomfortable feeling to see the red flame through the ice under me."

Another danger faced by the ship was the shallowness of the waters of the Northwest Passage. *St. Roch* grounded several times on her various voyages, and was lucky to get free. Because of this, another important position on the ship was a small platform, known as the "sounding deck," that projected out from the starboard side of the bow. Crewmembers were stationed there on six-hour shifts with an eight-pound lead weight attached to a lead line. The man's job was to swing the lead, "the heaviest eight pounds in the world," according to Bill White, far enough forward so that the ship's movement would straighten it out for an accurate reading of the depth of the water when the lead hit bottom. It was tedious and tiring work but very important. In 1935, when *St. Roch* sailed through a little-used passage, the crewman on the lead line sounded every two to three minutes to make sure the schooner did not run aground. In uncertain waters, the motor launch was sent ahead to sound, and if there was enough water, *St. Roch* followed. In this slow, ancient but safe-and-sure fashion, *St. Roch* survived 16 years in the Arctic.

St. Roch sailed from Fort Ross on September 2, reaching the RCMP detachment at Pond Inlet four days later. There they unloaded most of the schooner's Arctic gear and the dogs, and Larsen and the crew prepared for the final push out of the Arctic and on to Halifax, Nova Scotia. After stopping at Corner Brook, Newfoundland, for temporary repairs to the engine, *St. Roch* arrived off Halifax harbour at 3:30 in the afternoon on October 11, 1942.

It was a strange world that greeted the Mounties — the harbour was filled with warships and merchant vessels gathering together to form convoys through the U-boat-infested waters to Britain. A corvette escorted *St. Roch* through the mine field that protected the harbour entrance, and the crew moored the schooner to Kings Wharf. Henry Larsen had accomplished a near-impossible task. "It had not been an easy trip," he later reported in his typically understated way. The three seasons he had spent on the passage were the worst he had ever seen, though, and "without hesitation I would say that most ships encountering the conditions we faced would have failed."

St. Roch *at the dock in Halifax in 1942, after her first transit of the Northwest Passage.* (VANCOUVER MARITIME MUSEUM)

Chapter Five

BACK HOME AGAIN

S*t. Roch* sailed in July 1943 for a brief provisioning voyage from Halifax to Pond Inlet. The crew, picked for the most part from Newfoundland fishing schooners, left *St. Roch* after the three-month voyage through rough seas. During the winter of 1943, while *St. Roch* remained in Halifax, Larsen made a few trips to Ottawa to get his orders for 1944. Commissioner Wood told him that once again he would enter the Arctic and "if possible try to return to Vancouver by a different route of the Northwest Passage. This time I said I would like to try the more northerly route, through Lancaster Sound and west to Melville Island and then across McClure Strait to Prince of Wales Strait. This was the real Northwest Passage, I felt, and it had never before been navigated." While heavy ice was a concern, the reefs and shallows that had plagued *St. Roch* in 1940, 1941 and 1942 would not be a problem.

In Halifax, *St. Roch* was modernized for the voyage home. At the naval dockyard, workers installed a new, more powerful engine and built a larger deckhouse. The new mission, like the previous trip, was kept a wartime secret, and Larsen had "a great deal of trouble getting all the work completed on the ship on time." With his veterans of 1940-1942 gone to other assignments, a new crew was picked. Two seasoned hands, Rudolph Johnson and Ole Andreasson, joined *St. Roch* and, in a stroke of good luck, Larsen managed to sign on two of his old crewmembers — Constable Bill Peters and Constable Pat Hunt, who was promoted to acting corporal for the voyage.

The rest of the crew were new hands. Radio operator Lloyd Russill was a technician who had never sent or received a message until he was at sea aboard *St. Roch*. Two Newfoundland fishermen, a young constable fresh out of training from the Regina Barracks, a 17-year-old lad hired away from the shipyard where *St. Roch*'s rigging was being worked on, and a cook from an RCAF Air-Sea rescue boat filled out the crew of ten. *St. Roch* sailed on July 19, but engine trouble forced her back to port. Repairs were effected and on the 22nd, the schooner once again cleared harbour. After a brief stop at Sydney for additional repairs, this time to the exhaust pipe, which ran hot and threatened to start a fire, *St. Roch* was finally on her way, late in the season, on July 26.

In his private journal, Larsen wrote, "Well here we are again not quite ready for the great adventure of again trying to make the North West Passage .... We must do all in our power to uphold Canada's claim to this section of the Arctic. To quote Stefansson the explorer (The Northwest Course of Empire) must be kept open. I feel very proud to think that this important mission has been assigned to me again, and I hope I shall be able to fulfil the task before me, to uphold Canada's claim to these valuable islands and bulwark for our northern frontiers. Canada and its people have adopted me as one of their own sons, and it's up to me to be worthy of such an honour."

Larsen sailed *St. Roch* up Baffin Bay, arriving at Lancaster Sound and Pond Inlet on August 13. After landing some supplies, Larsen hired an Inuit guide and hunter, Joe Panipakuttuk, who came aboard with his six-member family and 17 dogs. "They were quite willing to sail with us and made themselves comfortable in a tent on top of our deck." Panipakuttuk and his family lived aboard *St. Roch* until the schooner reached Herschel Island, where Larsen put them ashore. In

Before the trip home, St. Roch's *new crewmembers pose on the deck in 1944 with Henry Larsen watching from the flying bridge.*
(VANCOUVER MARITIME MUSEUM)

addition to hunting, the Inuit were helpful in other ways. Crewmember Jim Diplock recalled that while working their way through the passage, "We weren't sure where we were." Joe's mother, Panipak, "looked at the coastline and checked with the chart. 'That's where we are,' she said. That's where we were!"

Three of the Inuit passengers were little girls: Anne Pallaq, a nine-year-old, eight-year-old Mary Panipakuttuk, and the "baby," four-year-old Soopi Viguq. Mary, interviewed in 1973, said, "I hated the trip. I was very young and I was always worried. The older people didn't worry but it was terrible living in the tent on the deck. The water would come right into the tent and I got scared." She wasn't alone. Joe Panipakuttuk, a man familiar with the sea and described by Henry Larsen as a "natural sailor," was horrified by the sea-keeping abilities of *St. Roch*. "The bow of the boat would disappear from time to time in the water. I was very frightened."

St. Roch sailed from Pond Inlet on August 17, and three days later anchored off Beechey Island, where three of Franklin's men were buried. Henry Larsen, an indefatigable Arctic scholar, went ashore with several of his crew to pay respects to the ill-fated expedition, explaining later, "I felt that I was on hallowed ground." Throughout the trip, Larsen stopped wherever possible to examine cairns, caches and other scattered remains left from the great age of Arctic exploration, and to collect a variety of relics. "Tribute is ... due to those early explorers," he said, because their "sacrifices and exploits blazed most of the trail we took." By the end of August, though, *St. Roch* stood off the entrance to McClure Strait. "We were now in waters never before sailed by any vessel," wrote Larsen, and he carefully worked his way into and across the strait, weaving through ice floes, and then south down Prince of Wales Strait.

On September 4, *St. Roch* passed Walker Bay, where the ship had wintered in 1940-1941, and anchored off Holman Bay. To all intents and purposes, the Northwest Passage had again been conquered. Larsen wired his arrival to headquarters, and was ordered to proceed

The Panipakuttuk family on deck, 1944. (ST. ROCH NHS)

to Vancouver. *St. Roch* now began a race with the ice. They rode out a savage winter storm at Tuk, "which we had reached just in time to save the ship." While initial reports of ice blocking the way out of the Arctic made it look as though the ship would have to winter at Tuk, the ice finally opened, and then slowly began to close in again. A quick dash was made to Herschel Island to land the Panipakuttuk family, and Larsen raced for Point Barrow.

Radio messages from Point Barrow indicated that a narrow lead remained open, but the shifting wind was closing it. "We could only go ahead, however, and I ordered the engineer to give her all she had. We simply had to make it, having come this far. The water shoaled alarmingly near the point when all of a sudden the leadsman, who had been kept busy without let-up, shouted, 'We've lost the bottom!'

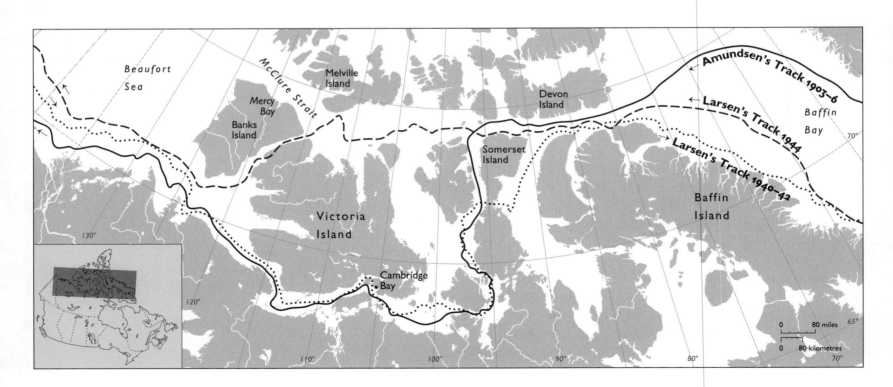

That was the call I had been waiting for; I now knew we had passed the point itself."

St. Roch passed through the Bering Strait on September 27, and a few weeks later was off the entrance to Vancouver harbour. The schooner tied up to the Evans, Coleman wharf in Vancouver at 6:00 P.M. on October 16. In an incredible feat, Henry Larsen had navigated the Northwest Passage — a distance of 7,295 miles — for the second time, in an amazing 86 days. The newspapers were full of the story, and Larsen, his crew and his ship were hailed and honoured by the city and the nation. For Henry Larsen, it meant a promotion to sub-inspector and the award of the Patron's Gold Medal by the Royal Geographical Society. The Royal Geographical Society also elected Larsen a Fellow, as did the Royal Canadian Geographical Society and the Arctic Institute of North America.

St. Roch returned to the Arctic in 1945-1946 under Henry Larsen's command. After a stop at Herschel Island to check on the welfare of Joe Panipakuttuk and his family, the schooner wintered at Cambridge Bay. The modern age had arrived and the majority of the crew was flown out of the Arctic for the winter. Troops participating in Operation Muskox, a combined Canadian-American military exercise testing Arctic survival gear, visited *St. Roch*, by now a symbol of an older, vanishing Arctic frontier. It was also a time of change for Henry Larsen; "The winter of 1945-46 also marked a watershed for me. It was my last aboard the *St. Roch*" in the Arctic. The schooner sailed from Cambridge Bay on August 12, and on the return voyage Larsen had the misfortune to anchor off Russian territory — Large Diomede Island — where the Russians arrested him and detained him overnight. *St. Roch* arrived back in Vancouver on September 26, 1946.

One last voyage north awaited the schooner in 1947. *St. Roch* halted at Herschel Island, from where most of the crew flew home for the winter. Larsen himself made a dog-sled trip to Aklavik, and then he too flew south for the holidays. When Larsen returned to *St. Roch* in the spring, he knew, as did his superiors, that the time had come to

Crewmember Billy Cashin on the bridge in 1944, at the end of St. Roch's second trip through the Northwest Passage.
(VANCOUVER MARITIME MUSEUM)

retire the schooner. "The Arctic, in short, was becoming 'civilized' and the *St. Roch* was out of her element in such surroundings," he wrote. The departure of the ship was a sad time for the Inuit, who came aboard for the last time on August 29, 1948. "The little ship had become a symbol of goodwill to all the Eskimos, this I know," Larsen later explained. "They knew we could be trusted to lend a helping hand, and no Eskimo, no matter what he had done, was ever afraid of coming to confide in us. They all knew that they would get fair treatment. Ours was not a police force to be afraid of."

St. Roch arrived in Vancouver on October 19, 1948. Retired and laid up in the naval dockyard in Esquimalt, her crew assigned to other duties, the veteran schooner was forgotten until 1950. That year, as the RCMP mulled over plans to reopen some of its detachments in the eastern Arctic, Henry Larsen, then commanding the RCMP's Arctic division, received permission to send *St. Roch* through the Panama Canal to Halifax under the command of Inspector Ken Hall, to support the RCMP's operations in the eastern Arctic. The trip from Vancouver to Halifax closed a loop that had started with the epic voyage of 1944; *St. Roch* was now the first vessel to circumnavigate North America.

Three weeks after transiting the canal, *St. Roch* sailed from Halifax on a five-month patrol to resupply RCMP detachments in Newfoundland and Labrador. The next year, the ship made her last operational voyage, a month-long Newfoundland patrol. She arrived back in Halifax on June 13, 1951, making fast alongside MacBrien Pier No. 1 at the dockyard.

Time and the ship's unique hull design now worked against *St. Roch*. The rounded, egg-shaped hull that served her so well in Arctic ice made *St. Roch* less than an ideal sailer in the more open waters of the eastern Arctic and Atlantic. As well, the ship still rolled and rocked and only made eight knots. Other, more modern, faster vessels were available for the resupply missions, so *St. Roch* remained alongside in the Halifax dockyard where the RCMP laid her up.

Chapter Six

PRESERVING A LEGACY

Far from home, *St. Roch* now faced a new danger — either rotting at the dock or being scrapped. Back in Vancouver, however, momentum built to place the vessel on permanent display. The RCMP sold *St. Roch* to the City of Vancouver, at Henry Larsen's urging, for $5,000; the price reflected the estimated cost of the fuel to bring the ship back to the west coast. With Larsen once again in command, *St. Roch* sailed south from Halifax on July 22, 1954, back through the canal, and up the Pacific coast to Vancouver, arriving on October 12, 1954.

"The welcome given the *St. Roch* ... was truly thrilling," wrote Larsen. "The huge new Royal Canadian icebreaker *Labrador* had arrived a few days previously .... We were given the honour of leading her into the harbour ... while craft from the Royal Vancouver Yacht Club manoeuvered into position, dipping their ensigns as we passed." It was an emotional moment for the skipper, who claimed, "One could almost feel the *St. Roch* quiver at the royal reception." The next day, in a ceremony at City Hall, the RCMP formally transferred *St. Roch* to the City of Vancouver. She lay idle at the Gore Avenue Wharf for the next four years as verbal battles raged over what to do with her. Former crewmember Rudolph Johnson served aboard as watchman.

St. Roch *at the Union Diesel plant in Oakland, California, on her final trip home in 1954.* (VANCOUVER MARITIME MUSEUM)

The new icebreaker Labrador *dwarfs the now-obsolete little* St. Roch *at Esquimalt in August 1954.* (VANCOUVER MARITIME MUSEUM)

St. Roch, *escorted by an honour guard of ships, passes beneath Vancouver's Lions Gate Bridge in 1958.* (PHOTOGRAPH BY BILL CUNNINGHAM, VANCOUVER *PROVINCE*)

In 1958 St. Roch *was beached in Haddon Park at the foot of Cypress Street; she had lain idle in Coal Harbour since 1954.* (VANCOUVER MARITIME MUSEUM)

"He pumps her out every day, but he seldom gets more than a gallon or so of water .... Once a week he lubricates the diesel engine and turns it over by hand. And he keeps a fire going, so she won't get musty or damp," reported the *Marine Digest* in July 1956.

In 1958, Vancouver Shipyards removed the 1944 deckhouse and restored the vessel's exterior to her 1928 appearance. On April 8, 1958, a heavy winch pulled *St. Roch* ashore on a cradle at Kitsilano Beach to serve as what the *Marine Digest* called "a symbolic cornerstone for this city's new maritime museum, being constructed as one of numerous projects in commemoration of the province's 100th anniversary." Construction of the Vancouver Maritime Museum was finished in 1959, but the schooner, resting inside a concrete drydock, remained in the open, slowly but steadily decaying.

The government recognized the national significance of *St. Roch* in 1962, when the Historic Sites and Monuments Board of Canada designated the ship a National Historic Site. In 1965, the federal government and the City of Vancouver entered into an agreement to preserve and interpret the story of *St. Roch*. In 1966, a $200,000 A-frame structure was built over the ship to protect her from the elements. In 1971, Parks Canada began a detailed, three-year restoration to return the ship to her 1944 appearance, which included a complete reconstruction of the deckhouse added to the ship in Halifax and scrapped in the first restoration in 1958. Repairs and replacement of some timbers in 1971 and 1972 also included sealing and reinforcing rotten timbers with fibreglass and replacing a large section of the deck. *St. Roch* reopened to the public on October 12, 1974, looking like her old self.

Parks Canada interpreters provided guided tours of the ship for the next 21 years. Work on the ship herself, now that she was enclosed in a building, was relegated to regular maintenance. All was well until the late 1980s, when leaks in the aging A-frame reactivated dry rot in the ship's timbers. Also, by 1990, Parks Canada realized that the ship's cradle, installed as a temporary support in 1958, was clearly failing. The preservation of a vessel out of water is difficult, since the water supports the hull, applying pressure equally to all points and helping the ship carry the weight of its engine and machinery. The wooden cradle and its few steel supports along the side of the hull had, over time, allowed *St. Roch* to settle unequally, twisting the timbers, opening seams and tearing at the hull, whose members were already weakened by dry rot from her many years in the open.

In the winter of 1991-1992, workers tore out the old cradle and replaced it with a new, all-steel support that better fit the contours of the ship and which, over the next decade, allowed the hull to settle back into shape. The City of Vancouver, working with Parks Canada, replaced the roof of the A-frame in 1992, stopping some of the leaks. But the aging building continued to leak at its end walls, allowing water in and keeping the dry rot fungus alive in many of the ship's timbers.

St. Roch suffered another setback in 1995 when Parks Canada, one of the key partners in the ship's preservation, closed *St. Roch* National Historic Site as a result of federal budget cutbacks. A grant of interim financing helped the ship through 1997, as did a commitment from the City of Vancouver to fund public access and tours of the ship. But the question of long-term preservation and the ultimate need for a new shelter required a plan for the future.

In 1997, the Vancouver Maritime Museum launched the *St. Roch* Preservation Campaign to start an endowment fund for the ship and to raise the money for a new shelter. The fund continues to grow, at a slow pace, while grants and sponsorships for specific programs and needs arrive each year. In 2001, the City of Vancouver rebuilt the leaking north wall of the shelter, reducing the number of leaks in the building to a minimum, while the Province of British Columbia funded a new series of exhibits to surround *St. Roch* and better tell the story of the ship and her crew.

The major initiative of the *St. Roch* Preservation Campaign was a two-year project, the *St. Roch II* Voyage of Rediscovery. After a year

When St. Roch *was partially restored, she was surrounded by a concrete dry dock; the new Vancouver Maritime Museum was built beside her.* (Vancouver Maritime Museum)

An A-frame structure was built over the ship in 1966 to protect her from the elements. (Photograph by Bill Cunningham, Vancouver Province)

and a half of planning, a modern, high-speed RCMP catamaran, *Nadon* (designated as *St. Roch II* for the voyage) set out from Vancouver to retrace *St. Roch*'s original route through the Northwest Passage. Their mission was not just to relive history, but to boldly blaze their own path through the north in a small, aluminum-hulled vessel built for coastal patrols. The goal of the voyage was simple and two-fold — to raise national and international awareness of the history and significance of *St. Roch* and to build up the permanent endowment fund for the ongoing preservation, maintenance, operation and interpretation of the ship.

Nadon/St. Roch II pulled away from Canada Place on the Vancouver waterfront on July 1, 2000, as flags whipped in the wind and an RCMP honour guard fired a volley of rifle shots into the sky. The six-month, 24,000-nautical-mile voyage, commanded by Sergeant Ken Burton of the RCMP, involved not just the catamaran and a rotating crew of RCMP officers, but also the Coast Guard icebreaker *Simon Fraser*, commanded by Captain Robert Mellis and a crew of volunteers from across Canada. Thousands bade the two ships bon voyage from Canada, and more than a million people followed the voyage via the World Wide Web. An on-board educator, Carolyn Dymond, made regular postings via the Internet to the interactive, bilingual web site, thanks to the Vancouver Foundation and the Vancouver School Board.

From Vancouver, *Nadon* and *Simon Fraser* headed up the coast, through the stormy Gulf of Alaska. Heavy seas pounded the tiny catamaran, just as they had hit *St. Roch* several decades earlier. *Nadon*'s tough aluminum hull survived, but more fragile electronics shorted out, leaving the ship without electrical power, radar or radio. The crew stood a continual watch for more than 48 hours, unable to sleep as the shallow-draft hull slammed into the waves. After temporary repairs, Burton and his crew headed north through an ice-free Bering Strait into the ice-choked Beaufort Sea. The pack ice blocked the way east, and several large ships stood by waiting for an opening, but

The dedication of St. Roch *as a museum vessel on June 11, 1959. (L to R) Rudolph Johnson, John Frederick, Henry Larsen, G.W. Peters, Joe Olsen.* (VANCOUVER MARITIME MUSEUM)

Burton, relying on his ship's shallow draft, ran in close to the shore, where the ice did not reach. His risky manoeuvre paid off when *Nadon* was the first vessel of the season to reach Tuk from the west. A number of observers who believed that the "ice is going to crush that boat like a beer can" were proved wrong.

Burton and Mellis, navigating along *St. Roch*'s original track from 1940-1942, made an ice-free transit of the Northwest Passage in a single month. To many observers, it was clear that the climate in the Arctic had changed since Larsen's day. As well, the entire north had changed. No longer the frontier that *St. Roch* had served, it is a series of communities and a land that has only recently been returned to Inuit self-government as the new territory of Nunavut, meaning "our land." There were ties to the past.

Along the way, the crew lived up to the original spirit of *St. Roch* by being more than just a police vessel. Scientists from the Institute of Ocean Sciences, near Victoria, made surveys from both ships. Archaeologists looked for traces of the lost Franklin expedition: Inuit guide Louie Kamookak showed Burton and his crew the skeletal remains and graves of some of Franklin's men on a small, isolated islet in the Todd Islands, just south of King William Island, but no other sign of Franklin or his ships emerged despite hours of slow examination of the seabed with sophisticated sonar.

However, Burton, Mellis and their crews made other important connections with the past. The two ships anchored at many of Larsen's old moorages, and in several communities Inuit elders talked about their memories of *St. Roch*, her crew and "Hanorie." At Taloyoak (Spence Bay), *Nadon*'s crew presented Special Constable Adam Totalik, one of Larsen's original guides, with a Long Service Medal. At Pasley Bay, the crew went ashore for a memorial service for Albert Chartrand and placed a large plaque with the RCMP crest on the cairn that marks the grave. At Pond Inlet, members of the Panipakuttuk family — including some who had sailed with Larsen in 1944 — came aboard for a tour. Descendants of *St. Roch*'s crew

First meeting of Nadon *and* Simon Fraser *in Vancouver.* (COURTESY OF SERGEANT KEN BURTON)

Nadon *at Smoking Hills, near the mouth of the Coppermine River.* (COURTESY OF SERGEANT KEN BURTON)

Constable John May *at the wheel.* (COURTESY OF SERGEANT KEN BURTON)

also sailed aboard *Nadon* and *Simon Fraser*, including Art Tomsett (1950-1951), Billy Cashin (1944-1948), Dean Hadley (1940-1942) and Hugh Parry, whose father, W.J. (Dad) Parry, sailed with Larsen from 1928 to 1934 and through the passage in 1940 to 1942. Henry Larsen's children, Gordon, Doreen and Beverly, as well as some of their children, also came aboard at key locations. Eager to join in, a number of retired members of the RCMP, many of whom had met or were inspired by Henry Larsen, also joined the crew and assisted at the two ships' many community visits.

The route largely avoided the Arctic's risks — ice, bad weather and the often extreme conditions at the top of the world — because it was a particularly warm summer. But two incidents reminded everyone of how dangerous this part of Canada still is. An Inuit hunting party whose boat had broken down was stranded on shore and Search and Rescue authorities asked *Nadon* to provide assistance. There was no one else to help and no other boat to turn to, so, despite heavy surf, the crew risked the landing to save the family. *Nadon*'s specially equipped Zodiac overturned and the crew was dumped into the frigid water off the barren and isolated Boothia Peninsula coast. The boat's operator, Corporal Mike Hartung, recovered the Zodiac and crew in the heavy surf and continued the mission, saving the hunters who were already suffering from exposure and lack of food after days in the open.

Another time, anchored for the night, *Nadon* went adrift when a small iceberg — the only ice in the vicinity — grounded on the catamaran's anchor chain and slowly dragged her into shoaling waters. As Burton and crew struggled to free the vessel, they had to face down an angry polar bear that stood on the ice, paws on *Nadon*. In the desperate attempt to push off and cut the anchor cable, crewmember Roger Kembel broke ribs when a pike pole slipped free of the ice and struck him.

The voyage through the Arctic ended, symbolically, on October 11, 2000, when *Nadon* moored at Halifax's Kings Wharf — exactly where *St. Roch* had tied up at the end of her first Northwest Passage transit — 58 years to the day from the original ship's arrival. Flying *St. Roch*'s original blue ensign, presented to the voyage by Doreen Larsen Riedel, who had cherished the flag as a special gift from her father, *Nadon* approached the wharf as the crowd cheered and the band struck up a welcome. It was a very different and more public welcome than the wartime, no-fuss entry of *St. Roch* on October 11, 1942.

From Halifax, *Nadon* retraced her predecessor's circumnavigation, running south along the Atlantic seaboard of the United States, through the Caribbean and the Panama Canal and up the Pacific coast. Returning to Canadian waters on December 14, 2000, *Nadon* tied up in front of the Vancouver Maritime Museum, in full view of *St. Roch*, in the middle of a freezing cold rainstorm on December 16. "Coldest day of the entire voyage," quipped Sergeant Burton.

The voyage was a unique opportunity that comes rarely, in which people, be they the crew, the volunteers or the public who watched, can experience a convergence of the past, present and future. Reawakened to the nationally significant

Inspector Don Saigle with the Zodiac. (COURTESY OF SERGEANT KEN BURTON)

story of *St. Roch*, governments, corporations and private individuals stepped forward to ensure the ship's ongoing preservation. Since the voyage was completed, the fund for the ship has grown, and gifts continue to come in. The task is not yet over, nor are the coffers full. More effort, and more support, is needed, but the task ahead is clear and the voyage's partners, particularly Alcan, TrendWest Resorts, the RCMP, the Canadian Coast Guard and the Millennium Bureau of Canada, as well as all the other sponsors and supporters, charted the way.

Why save this ship? Because she is much more than an artifact. *St. Roch* is an embodiment of important values: sacrifice, perseverance, teamwork and pursuing a dream despite the risks and the potential cost. These values are passed on through the example of the ship and her crew, and are essential lessons for children, as well as reminders of what defines some of the best aspects of the human heart. The story of *St. Roch*, without the ship, would in time become just that — a story, a legend, a dimly remembered footnote or a dusty photograph. But to tour *St. Roch*, to walk the decks and venture inside the crowded forecastle and cabins, brings the story alive.

The vessel looks exactly the way she did during the 1944 voyage, with clothing hanging from hooks, reading material on bunks, supplies in the hold, a calendar on the engine-room bulkhead and the tent and belongings of Joe Panipakuttuk and his family on the hatch cover. Taped radio broadcasts and the sounds of creaking ice and howling dogs increase the sense of what it was like. Enshrined ashore beneath glass, *St. Roch* no longer plows the Arctic seas. Yet she offers all who visit her a firsthand look at a unique vessel, her contribution to Canadian and world maritime history and the men who served aboard.

Nadon *under way.* (COURTESY OF SERGEANT KEN BURTON)

Chapter Seven

ANATOMY OF A SHIP

Burrard Dry Dock built *St. Roch* of native Douglas fir. The double-sawn frames, on 20-inch centres, measure 13 by 7 inches in the floors and 7 by 7 inches molded and sided at the first futtock. The hull is planked with 2¾-inch Douglas fir outer-hull planks and 3½-inch-thick ceiling planks. One timber of each frame carries up to form the bulwark stanchions. The hull is heavily fastened with galvanized iron drifts and bolts clenched over galvanized washers. The 11½-by-14-inch keel, the 10-by-16-inch stem and the 11-by-15-inch sternpost, as well as the rubrail and caprail, are made of ironbark (Australian gumwood). The deck is made of 6½-inch-wide, 3-inch-thick Douglas fir planks attached to the beams with galvanized screws and covered with plugs.

The outer hull is sheathed with inch-and-a-half-thick ironbark planks. The ironbark planks have gaps between them, and were not caulked, to allow the seawater to reach the Douglas fir hull and prevent dry rot. The rudder is also ironbark and could be winched to the deck through a well at the stern. Ironbark is strong, but heavy, and if the rudder came loose it would sink, so an extra rudder was always kept ready, stowed on deck. In addition to the thick hull planks, the ship carried extra sheathing at the bow to fend off the ice. Originally, 3/8-inch-thick steel plate protected the bow. In 1940,

the RCMP replaced this with a new ½-inch-thick steel shoe described by Henry as "very sharp instead of almost a foot across, as it had been."

The ship has an elevated poop and forecastle deck, with breaks. The hull was originally dark grey with white trim, but in or around 1930 the schooner was painted white with grey trim. By 1939 or 1940 the RCMP restored the ship's original colour scheme. *St. Roch* is now in her 1944 scheme of dark grey hull with black trim, with red bottom paint below the waterline. The decks, always painted with red oxide, remain that colour today.

Thomas Halliday designed the ship with a round hull to protect *St. Roch* from the crushing pressure of ice floes. The hull is shaped like an egg, for strength and to create a surface that cannot easily be gripped or caught, so that the ship would roll out of the ice. While this worked well in the ice, in heavy seas *St. Roch* "heaved and bucked like a bronco," as one seasick Mountie gasped to Henry Larsen on the maiden voyage. It was an apt analogy for the RCMP crew, who had been kidded with the name "horse sailors" on the Vancouver waterfront. To strengthen the hull, 11½-inch, horizontal "strong" or ice beams supported the weather deck and braced the hold, while iron hanging knees and wooden lodging knees with iron reinforcing supported the beams. Ordinary deck beams ranged from 5½ to 7 inches. The space between the floors was filled with cement, which was a standard shipbuilding practice at the time. *St. Roch* survived several near-crushings in the ice because of her hull.

As an auxiliary schooner, *St. Roch* sported a full fore-and-aft rig on her two masts. The schooner carried three sails: the mainsail, foresail and the staysail or "jumbo." A crow's-nest, or "ice-bucket" as it was called in the Arctic, hung suspended from the mainmast for the lookout. The standing rigging was wire rope attached to bar chainplates with turnbuckles, while the running rigging was the traditional hemp.

In addition to sails, *St. Roch* originally carried a single, 150-horsepower, marine diesel engine manufactured by the Union Diesel Engine Company of Oakland, California, and installed by Burrard Iron Works of Vancouver. The engine, with a sailing clutch to disengage the shaft and let the propeller spin free, hence reducing drag when the schooner was under sail, drove a single, three-bladed bronze screw. Larsen asked that this be replaced in 1935 with a new screw, and that one in turn was replaced in 1945 with a four-bladed screw. The vibration caused by the new propeller was too much, though, and the three-bladed screw was reinstalled. The four-bladed propeller, retained as a spare, stills rests on the aft deck. In 1943, workers in Halifax replaced the original engine with a larger, 18-ton, 300-horsepower Union diesel, the engine that remains aboard to this day.

The engine room also accommodated an eight-horsepower Union gas motor that served as an auxiliary compressor; it charged the two riveted-steel tanks used to air-start the diesel engine and a 22-kilowatt generator. This small motor was also used to pump water. Since there were no batteries, electrical power was available only when the motor was running; to conserve fuel during the long winters, the motor was not run often, and then it was usually to power the wireless. *St. Roch*'s crew relied on kerosene lamps for light. In 1940, when the ship was refitted for her first voyage through the Northwest Passage, the naval dockyard at Esquimalt added another auxiliary, an 18-horsepower Russel Newbury diesel motor, to charge a small rack of batteries.

St. Roch carried eight fuel tanks — two 1,750-gallon tanks abeam of the engine, four 850-gallon tanks, one atop the other on each beam immediately aft of the forecastle, a 50-gallon feed tank near the diesel engine to supply its needs, and a 150-gallon "distillate tank" with gasoline for the auxiliary motor. *St. Roch* also carried a thousand-gallon fresh-water tank in the hold beneath the forecastle. Mindful of his need for fuel in the isolated Arctic, Larsen had the naval dockyard at Halifax add additional fuel tanks in the stern in 1944. The ship did not carry a great deal of fuel; records from 1950 indicate

St. Roch *in her original configuration of 1928 as an open-decked auxiliary schooner with a small deckhouse.* (VANCOUVER MARITIME MUSEUM)

that her fuel capacity was 7,000 gallons, but this did not count fuel stowed in 45-gallon barrels on the deck or in the hold, nor the caches of fuel barrels at strategically placed depots throughout the Arctic. The engine burned 290 gallons of oil a day, making the extra fuel a necessity on long Arctic voyages. Crewmember Jack Foster later recalled, "At one time, we had 40,000 gallons of diesel fuel scattered in various caches around the western Arctic coast."

The schooner's tackle and furniture included two forged, stockless best bower anchors, 7¼ CWT (hundredweight) each, with shanks 12 inches longer than usual, a 2-CWT stream anchor and 2 ice anchors. After the 1928 maiden voyage, Larsen added a 700-pound kedge anchor to the ship's equipment. There were two engine-powered windlasses, one on the weather deck and the other on the forecastle head. In 1930, Vancouver's Terminal City Ironworks replaced the original anchor windlass with a stronger one manufactured by them. Two wire-rope reels were added later to assist in moving cargo and pulling the ship through the ice. The chain locker held 90 fathoms of 7/8-inch stud-link chain. The boatswain's stores included 180 fathoms of 3¼-inch rope, 45 fathoms of 2¼-inch rope, 75 fathoms of six-inch manila and 90 fathoms of 4-inch hawser. The ship's pumps were cast by Pumps and Power, Ltd., of Vancouver. *St. Roch* was originally equipped with an 18-foot Class I lifeboat and a 20-foot motorboat; these were later augmented by a 12-foot pram, a 12-foot punt and a 20-foot square-ended cargo scow that were stowed on the weather deck. Davits for cargo and the spare boats were installed aft, at the bow and, in 1944, amidships.

St. Roch accommodated 13 men and approximately 100 to 150 tons of cargo when she was built, and sailed with 10 crew. The men who lived in the forecastle reached it through a small companionway, and gained access to the hold, where cargo and supplies were stowed, through an 8-by-12-foot main hatch. The forecastle held six berths, lockers, a mess table and a Number 12, coal-fired Viking Quebec stove for warmth. The main cabin aft, below the weather deck, was

St. Roch *re-rigged as a ketch in 1944, with a larger deckhouse.*
(VANCOUVER MARITIME MUSEUM)

accessible through a trunk and ladder abaft the deckhouse; it had four berths with drawers under them, settees and a folding mess table. The captain was accommodated in the deckhouse. Forward of the main cabin were two smaller cabins: to port was the galley, with a coal-fired range; to starboard was the wireless office. The accommodations were small and cramped. According to Henry Larsen, "*St. Roch* was, and remained, the most uncomfortable ship I have ever been in."

Hatches from all three cabins opened into a trunk that led below the engine room. Aft of the main cabin was a smaller space for the head to port and cook's stores to starboard. The lazarette was taken up with boatswain's stores. The deckhouse, located just aft of the mainmast, was divided into the wheelhouse and the captain's cabin with a head, and the trunk leading to the main cabin at the aft end. The original deckhouse leaked badly and warped on the maiden voyage, so in 1930 the RCMP replaced it with a slightly larger deckhouse, with a small cabin added aft of it for the wireless, and an officer's cabin beside the captain's. In 1935, an open navigating bridge was built atop the pilothouse, and an engine-room telegraph was installed for the first time. Before this, all communication with the engine room had been by bells; this led to confusion when the signals flew fast and furious as the ship was dodging ice floes.

Larsen had the opportunity to make the first major improvements to the vessel in August 1944 during the refit at the naval dockyard at Halifax. The dockyard replaced the original diesel engine, removed the windlass on the weather deck and after the engine's installation built a new, larger deckhouse. During this work, the yard removed the mainmast as it was in the way of the new deckhouse, and added a shorter mizzenmast near the stern; "In this way, we could carry a small riding, or storm sail there," explained Larsen. "This was an alteration I had in mind a long time." Now rigged as a ketch, *St. Roch* carried reduced sail. Except for rare circumstances, the ship never sailed anyway.

CHARACTERISTICS OF ST. ROCH

Length Overall: 104 feet, 3 inches
Waterline: 97 feet, 6 inches
Between perpendiculars: 95 feet
Beam: 24 feet, 9 inches
Draft (loaded): 12½ to 13 feet
Depth: molded 11 feet at the stern, 9 feet, 6 inches
    at the bow
Height of mainmast: 62 feet, 3 inches
Height of foremast: 56 feet
Height of mizzenmast (1944): 39 feet
Sail Area:
    Mainsail: 1,185 square feet (1928), 456 square feet
      (1944)
    Foresail: 830 square feet
    Staysail: 420 square feet (1928), 336 square feet
      (1944)
    Mizzen: 346 square feet
Displacement: 323 tons
Registered at 193.43 tons gross, 80.60 tons net
Engine (1928-1943): 150-h.p. Union diesel, 6-cylin-
    der, 4-cycle, single acting, 8¾-inch-diameter cyl-
    inders, 340 r.p.m.
Engine (1944-): 300-h.p. Union diesel, 6-cylinder,
    4-cycle, 11-inch-diameter cylinders, 350 r.p.m.
Propeller: Single screw, three blades, 58 inches in di-
    ameter, with a 35-inch pitch.

In all, the skipper was pleased. "With a new deckhouse the *St. Roch* had a new look and certainly was more efficient than before." The new deckhouse covered much of the poop deck and supported an elevated pilothouse, which in turn had an open navigating bridge atop it. This change greatly improved operations, since the original pilothouse had not had a clear line of sight over the bow and the helmsman had had to rely on observations shouted from the mainmast. A new ice-bucket was rigged below the truck of the foremast.

Aft of the pilothouse, a skylight and the funnel occupied the top of the deckhouse along with the two boats. Small cabins arranged around a central trunk accommodated Larsen, the engineer, the mates, the wireless, the galley (with a new oil-fired Atlantic range) and a lounge. The rest of the crew was berthed in the forecastle, which included a few spare bunks for visitors. *St. Roch* could now comfortably carry 15 persons, although on the 1944 voyage she was crowded with 19. The original main cabin below deck held enlarged cook's stores, reserve fuel tanks and a new battery room for 561.5-volt cells stored on three racks, which meant that electricity was available more often and could be obtained without running the auxiliary motor. Also below, and added in 1944, was a naval gyro compass for navigating in the fluctuating magnetic currents of the north where no ordinary compass would function.

With the exception of minor repairs, such as the replacement of 33 feet of false keel and a foot of the main keel in 1930 after *St. Roch* ran aground on her first trip north, plus the new deckhouse of 1930 and the relatively few modifications made in 1935 and 1940, the ship remained basically unaltered until 1944, and thereafter operated unchanged in the service of the RCMP until her retirement. In the 30 years between her launch and going ashore to be preserved, the plucky little schooner lived up to her reputation as "a tough ship." *St. Roch* survived groundings and collisions with icebergs, in a rough and rugged career afloat, a tribute both to her builders and to the skill of the men who served aboard her.

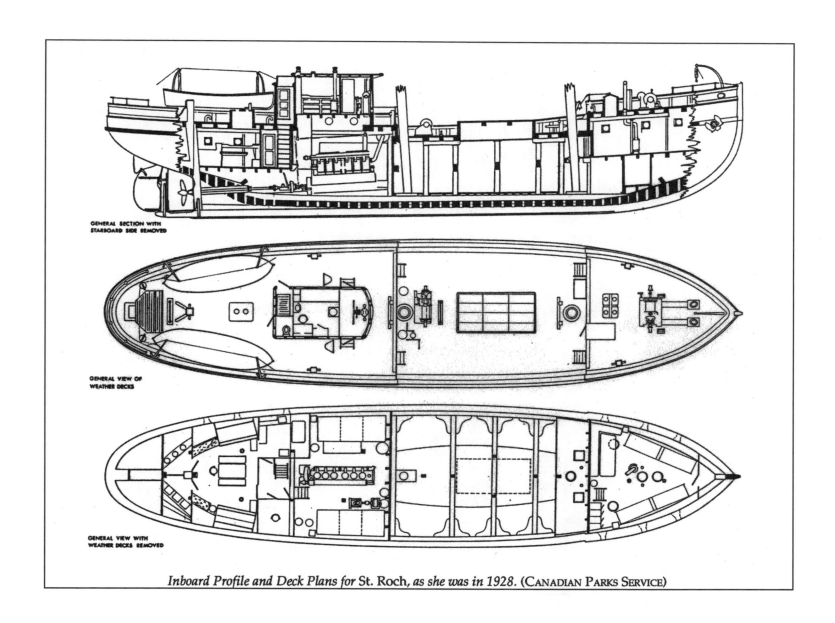

GENERAL SECTION WITH
STARBOARD SIDE REMOVED

GENERAL VIEW OF
WEATHER DECKS

GENERAL VIEW WITH
WEATHER DECKS REMOVED

Inboard Profile and Deck Plans for St. Roch, as she was in 1928. (CANADIAN PARKS SERVICE)

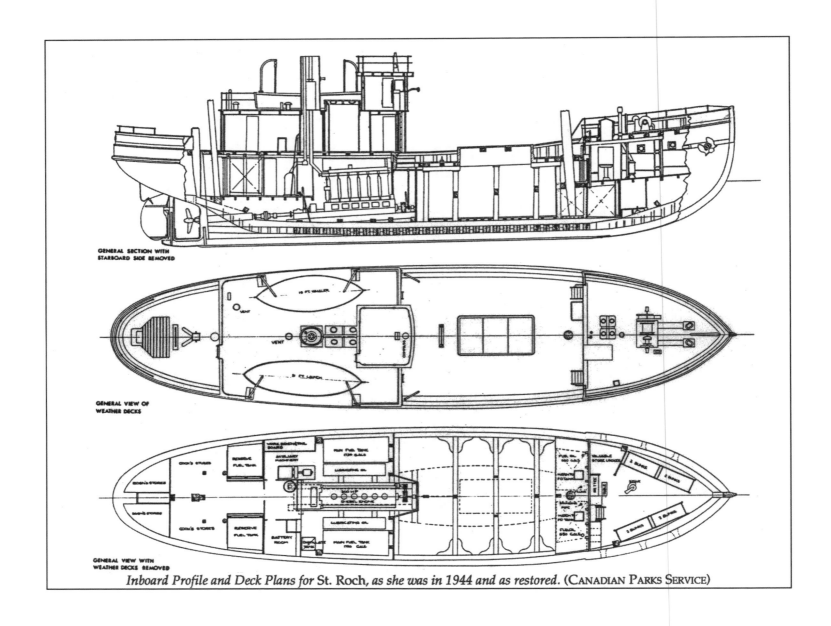

GENERAL SECTION WITH
STARBOARD SIDE REMOVED

GENERAL VIEW OF
WEATHER DECKS

GENERAL VIEW WITH
WEATHER DECKS REMOVED

Inboard Profile and Deck Plans for St. Roch, as she was in 1944 and as restored. (CANADIAN PARKS SERVICE)

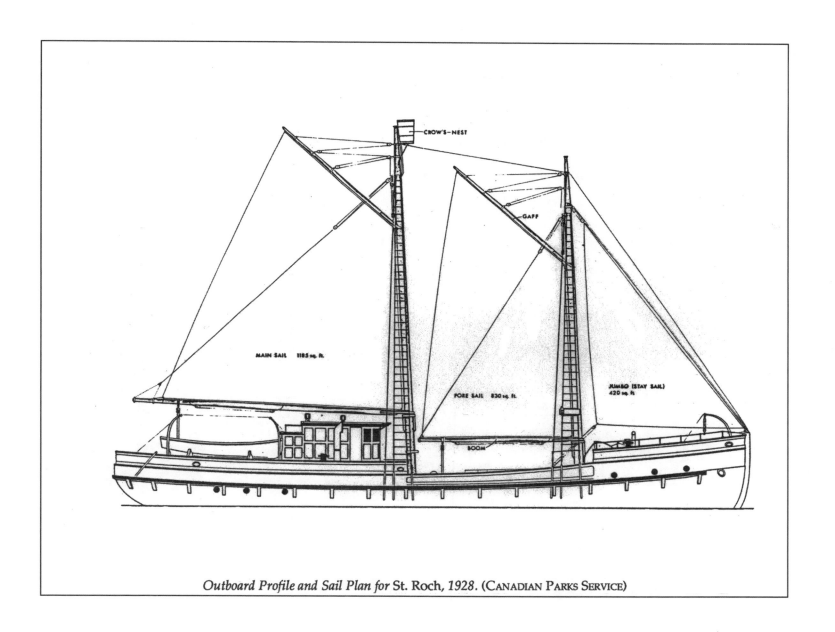

CROW'S-NEST

GAFF

MAIN SAIL 1185 sq. ft.

FORE SAIL 830 sq. ft.

JUMBO (STAY SAIL) 420 sq. ft.

BOOM

Outboard Profile and Sail Plan for St. Roch, 1928. (CANADIAN PARKS SERVICE)

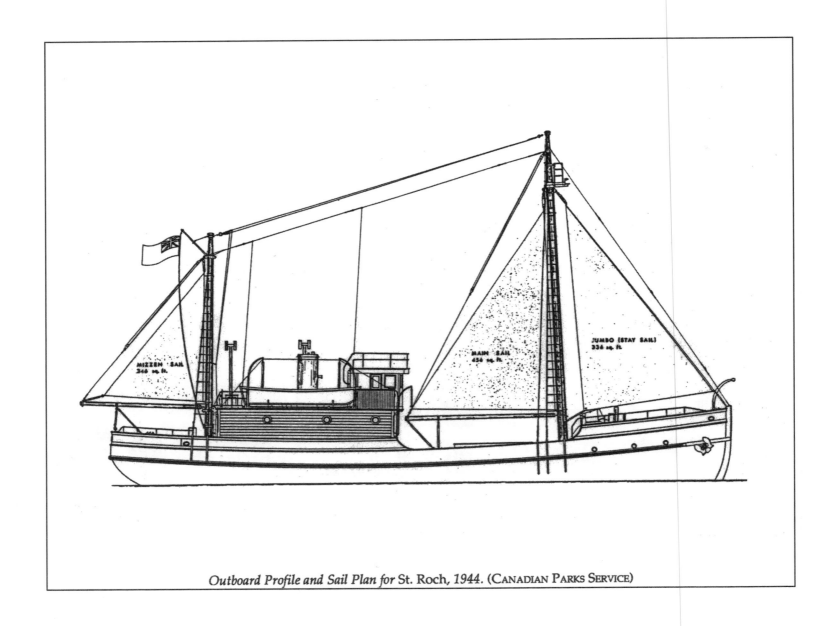

MIZZEN SAIL
346 sq. ft.

MAIN SAIL
456 sq. ft.

JUMBO (STAY SAIL)
336 sq. ft.

Outboard Profile and Sail Plan for St. Roch, 1944. (CANADIAN PARKS SERVICE)

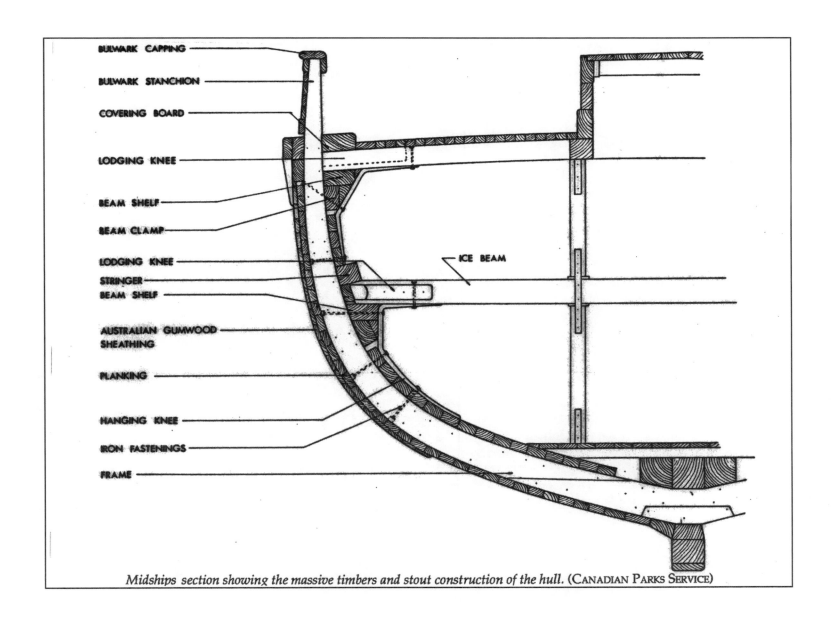

BULWARK CAPPING

BULWARK STANCHION

COVERING BOARD

LODGING KNEE

BEAM SHELF

BEAM CLAMP

LODGING KNEE

STRINGER

BEAM SHELF

AUSTRALIAN GUMWOOD
SHEATHING

PLANKING

HANGING KNEE

IRON FASTENINGS

FRAME

ICE BEAM

Midships section showing the massive timbers and stout construction of the hull. (Canadian Parks Service)

Appendix One
CHRONOLOGY OF ST. ROCH'S VOYAGES

1928-29: The maiden voyage and *St. Roch*'s first into the Canadian Arctic. The schooner sailed from Vancouver on June 28, 1928, wintered at Langton Bay, and returned in the fall of 1929.

1930-34: The longest voyage in the history of the ship. *St. Roch* provided service to the Coronation Gulf area of the western Arctic. Returned to Vancouver after spending four winters there.

1935-37: *St. Roch* wintered at Cambridge Bay for two years.

1938-39: Sent once again to Cambridge Bay, *St. Roch* returned to Vancouver with the outbreak of World War II.

1940-42: Historic 28-month voyage through the Northwest Passage from west to east. *St. Roch* arrived at Halifax on October 11th, 1942.

1943: A three-month voyage of supply to RCMP detachments in the eastern Arctic.

1944: *St. Roch*'s "lucky" 86-day voyage on the more northerly route of the Northwest Passage from east to west, sailing from Halifax to Vancouver.

1945-46: A post-war voyage to Cambridge Bay. *St. Roch* was visited by Operation Muskox, and on the return, Captain Larsen was arrested and detained overnight by the Russians when he anchored off Large Diomede Island.

1947-48: *St. Roch*'s last Arctic voyage, supplying the RCMP detachments in the western Arctic. The ship wintered at Herschel Island, but most of the crew were flown out for Christmas. On her return to Vancouver, *St. Roch* was laid up.

1950-51: *St. Roch* sailed from Vancouver to Halifax by way of the Panama Canal, becoming the first ship to circumnavigate North America. The ship made one voyage to the northern regions of Hudson Bay.

1954: With Henry Larsen in command, *St. Roch* returned to Vancouver by way of the Panama Canal for preservation as a museum vessel.

Appendix Two
MEMBERS OF THE CREW

This partial list of the crew, prepared by the staff of *St. Roch* National Historic Site, also provides the dates by year that each man served aboard. Some members of the RCMP, as well as civilians and other government personnel, did travel aboard *St. Roch*, but did not appear in Parks Canada's official crew list and hence are not listed here.

Legend

Insp. = Inspector
Cst. = Constable
Sp. Cst. = Special Constable
S/Cst. = Sub-Constable
Cpl. = Corporal
Sgt. = Sergeant
emp. civ. = employed civilian
*First trip through the Northwest Passage
**Second trip through the Northwest Passage
***Both trips through the Northwest Passage
^ Circumnavigated North America
+Constable Albert Chartrand was the only member of *St. Roch*'s crew to die in the line of duty.

Ackles, K.C. S/Cst. 1945-47
Alexander, Scott F. Cst. 1935-37
Anderton, Frederick (Andy) Sgt. 1928-33
Andreasson, Ole Sp. Cst. 1944**
Angulalik, guide, Queen Maud Gulf
Atkins, C.W. S/Cst. 1951
Aucherlonie, G. Tom 1947-48
Bayers (Byers?), R.W. S/Cst. 1954
Beattie, R. S/Cst. 1948
Bell, Clarence
Blair, J.R. Cst. 1949
Blues, D.F. 1932-34
Boutilier, B.G. Cst. 1950-51

Boutilier, John T. emp. civ. 1943-44**
Braun, W.A. S/Cst. 1954
Brunner, P.A. S/Cst. 1954
Budge (Bridge?), A.M. 1948
Burton, J.R. Cst. 1948-50
Byer, Stan S/Cst. 1948
Carter, W.S. Cst. 1932-33
Cashin, William M. Sp. Cst. 1944, 1948**
Chaisson, Victor D. S/Cst. 1954
Chartrand, Albert J. Cst. 1938-1941*+
Cheetham, John R. Cst. 1935-36
Christie, R.W. Cst. 1939
Clark, C.B. Sp. Cst. 1946
Coffin, Gordon L. Cpl. 1947-48
Collen, Walter V. Cst. 1947
Cooper, J.B. S/Sgt. 1950-51
Cranney, J.J. Cst. 1933-34, 1936-37
Cresine, H.E.B. Cst. 1938
Dauphinee, C. S/Cst. 1954
Davies, James H. Cst. 1930, 1933-34
Deveau, J.W. S/Cst. 1950
Develin, D. S/Cst. 1951
Dickens, G.B. Sp. Cst. 1944**
Diplock, James M. S/Cst. 1944**
Douthwaite, C.R.R. Cst. 1935-37
Dowden, C.H. S/Cst. 1951
Doyle, Jack Cst. 1942
Driscoll, W.F. S/Cst. 1951
Duffy, Maurice G. Cst. 1947
Duke, John E. Sp. Cst. 1930-33
Dunn, T.B. Cst. 1949
Eddy, J.U. 1936-37
Eisenhauer, I.H. Cst. 1948
Farrar, Fred S. Cst. 1930-34, 1938-43, 1950* ^
Fielder, L.F. Cst. 1930
Fleet, B.W. A/Cst. 1945
Foster, M.F. Cst. 1928-34, Cpl. 1938-42*
Friederich, James Cst. 1940
Gillen, W. H. delivery captain, 1928

Gingell, J.N. S/Cst. 1950-51
Goodey, Reginald J. Cst. 1935, 1938-39
Green, R.W. Cst. 1940
Hadley, Edward (Dean) Cst. 1940-42*
Hall, Chipman
Hall, K.W.N. Insp. 1950
Henderson, F.J.J. Sgt. 1950-51
Holt, H. Sp. Cst. 1930
Hull, D. S/Cst. 1954
Humphrey, H.C. Cst. 1937
Hunt, Patrick G. Cst. 1940-42, 1944-47***
Jacobsen, Fred pilot 1928
Jennings, S.G. S/Cst. 1954
Johnson, D.J. S/Cst. 1944, 1947-48, 1950-51
Johnson, Rudolph T. Sp. Cst. 1943-49**
Jones, P.W. Cst. 1947, 1951
Josephson, V.R. Cst. 1938,1939
Kane, G.F. S/Cst. 1951
Keating, Mike P. Sp. Cst. 1943-49**
Kells, Robert W. Cst. 1928-37
Kelly, Pat delivery engineer 1928
Knickle, W.E.D. emp. civ. 1943
Kujuluu, guide
LaBreche, G.F. Cst. 1951
Lamb, L.R. S/Cst. 1954
Lamothe, A. Cst. 1928
Larsen, Henry A. Captain 1928-48, 1954*** ^
Lavoie, J.F.H. A. Cst. 1935-36
Lemieux, J.S. S/Cst. 1945
Lohnes, K.K. emp.civ. 1943
Luke, M. S/Cst. 1936
MacKenzie, Alec Cst. 1935-36
MacPherson, C.S. Sgt. 1950-
MacRae, Jack A. 1931-32, 1934
Makinson, George T. Cpl. 1933-36
Malik, guide
Margetts, J.V. Cst. 1947
Marshal, William E. Cst. 1944**
Matthews, Frank S/Cst. 1944**

Mayo, H. (Ted) emp. civ. 1943-44**
McKenzie, J.Stanley S/Cst. 1944**
Menzies, G.S. S/Cst. 1951, 1954
Mercier, F.J.J. emp. civ. 1943
Monette, Joseph J. Cst. 1950
Moore, G.P.C. Cst. 1937
Moore, G.T. (Dinty) Cst. 1930-32
Mossman, H.V. S/Sgt. 1954
Mott, Wilfred H. Cst. 1948-51, 1954
Norris, H.A. Cst. 1951
Nutt (possibly Mott), W.H. Cst. 1954
Olsen, M.J. Cst. 1928-30
Owen-Jones, A.H. 1930-32
Owens, Mitch 1944
Panipakuttuk, Joe guide 1944
Paniujakak, David interpreter 1944, 1946
Parke, Willis V. emp. civ. 1943-44**
Parkes, Derek E. Cst. 1938-39
Parry, W.J. (Dad) Cst. 1928-34, 1940-42**
Parsloe, T.G. (Terry) Cst. 1928
Pearo, L.P. Cst. 1946-48
Perks, D. Cpl. 1934
Peters, G.W. (Bill) Cst. 1938, 1940-47, 1949***
Piccott, G.T. S/Cst. 1951
Pigeon, Clarence L. S/Cst. 1945

Porter, G.M. emp. civ. 1941
Powell, R.N. S/Cst. 1951
Reed, W.C.G. Sp. Cst. 1946
Reid, A.E. S/Cst. 1950-51, 1954
Roberts, N.C. Cpl. 1951
Rushton, E.S. S/Cst. 1951
Russill, Lloyd G. Sp. Cst. 1944**
Sargent, Glen Kirk Cst. 1947-48
Sealey, Fred W. Sp. Cst. 1928-29
Shaw, W.C. S/Cst. 1954
Smith, F.M. Cpl. 1950
Smith, Laurence C. S/Cst. 1945-46
Smith, Murray S/Cst. 1947 (1950-51?)
Stevenson, J.L. S/Cst. 1951
Tieleman, Harry W. S/Cst.
Tomsett, Arthur F. Cst. 1950-51
Tremaine, J.W.H. Cpl. 1951
Tudor, A. Frank C. 1928
Wall, G.M. Cpl. 1933
Wareham, G.T. Cst. 1939
Welsh, Thomas F.D. Cst. 1935-37
White, L.W.L. (Bill) Cst. 1930, 1934
Willan, L. Frank Cst. 1935-37
Wilson, A.S. Cpl. 1943
Wood, C.E. Cst. 1929-30, 1934-37

Appendix Three
MEMBERS OF THE CREW OF ST. ROCH II
VOYAGE OF REDISCOVERY

RCMP *Nadon/St. Roch II*
- Burton, David
- Burton, Ken Sgt. Officer in Command
- Clarke, Ann Cpl.
- Cochlan, Dan Cst.
- Cunha, Vic Cst.
- Currie, Bob Cpl.
- Gates, Ken Insp.
- Harry, Richard Cst.
- Hartung, Michael Cpl.
- Haycock, Ken Cst.
- Henley, John Insp.
- Kembel, Roger Insp.
- Lalear, Frank Sgt.
- May, John Cpl.
- Ouellette, Bruno Cpl.
- Pinnegar, Gene Sgt.
- Saigle, Don Insp.
- Sauvé, Jasmin (engineer)
- Schmiesser, Mike Cst.
- Soo, Jack (engineer)
- Stringer, John Cst.
- Van Dusen, Don

Archaeological Survey
- Delgado, James P.
- Hobson, George
- Treverrow, Mark
- Woodman, David

Simon Fraser
- Asselin, Jacques Chief Engineer
- Bedocs, Laslo Oiler: Arctic
- Bragg, Jack Capt. Second Officer: Panama

- Dancer, W. Capt. Second Officer: Arctic
- Eberlein, Frank Oiler: Panama
- Erlam, James Seaman
- Ferguson, Doreen Steward: Panama
- Ferguson, Michael Seaman: Panama
- Forbes, Dr. Francis (Blackie) Medical Officer
- Franks, Naomi Steward: Arctic
- Gibbins, Amie Seaman
- Gillis, Gordon Chief Cook
- Isserlis, Paul Boatswain: Arctic
- Johns, David Capt. Director of Support Operations
- Landry, Bruce Boatswain: Panama, Seaman: Arctic
- Lyngard, Jack 1st Engineer: Panama
- MacDougal, James 3rd Engineer
- Malacarne, Peter Steward: Arctic
- Martens, Oscar Seaman: Arctic
- McKay, Moody Third Officer
- Mellis, C. Capt. Chief Officer
- Mellis, Capt. R. J. Master
- Mont, Mike Seaman: Arctic
- Parry, Hugh Electrician
- Patrick, Rena Steward: Arctic
- Provost, Thea Second Cook
- Roberts, Lyle Oiler: Panama
- Robinson, Bill Oiler: Arctic
- Rooney, John Seaman: Panama
- Sauvé, Diane Engineering Cadet: Arctic
- Sauvé, Jasmin Oiler: Arctic (later transferred to *Nadon*)
- Sharp, Sue Seaman
- Simms, Dianne Bosun's Mate
- Syomin, Vlodomir 1st Engineer: Arctic
- Tomsett, Art 2nd Engineer
- Weber, Allan Oiler: Panama
- Wood, Margo Steward: Panama

Voyage of Rediscovery Project Personnel, Vancouver
- Delgado, James P.
- Fitzgerald, Katie
- Johansen, Gina

Knight, Tara
Rybak, Stephen
Virani, Salima

Voyage of Rediscovery Project Steering Committee
Carmak, Edward
Davies, Don
Defieux, Ron
Delgado, James P.
Grant, John

Hobson, George
Holmes, Les
Johns, David
Kembel, Roger
Morris, Linda
Palmer, Frank
Saigle, Don
Valpy, David
Watt, Brian

Glossary

Abaft: To the rear of, behind or toward the stern of the ship.

Aft: In, near, or toward the stern of the ship.

Beam Ends: A ship is on her beam ends when she lies on her sides so that the deck beams are vertical.

Boatswain or Bosun: A petty officer aboard ship, in charge of the deck crew. The boatswain's locker is a compartment used to store small tools and gear for working with the ship's rigging.

Bower: The largest anchors aboard ship, carried at the bow.

Bulwark: The sides of the ship that project above the deck to form a fence or railing.

Caprail: The timber that caps the bulwark.

Chainplates: Metal strips attached to the side of the hull, to which the rigging that supports the mast is attached.

Drift: A metal pin that holds together timbers in a wooden ship.

Floors: The frames at the bottom of the ship near the keel.

Forecastle or Fo'c'sle: A compartment at the bow of the ship where the crew have their bunks.

Foremast: The mast at the forward end of a ship, the mast closest to the bow.

Frames: The ribs of a ship.

Futtock: The pieces that when joined together make a single frame, or rib of a ship.

Ketch: A two-masted, fore-and-aft rig similar to that of a schooner except that the largest sails are carried on the foremast, which is also taller than the mizzenmast; the opposite is true for a schooner rig.

Knees: Naturally grown timbers in the shape of a bracket that support the deck beams or brace other timbers in a wooden ship. Some knees are made of iron or steel.

Lazarette: A small space or compartment below deck at the stern of a ship, used to store provisions.

Lead: An opening in pack ice that a ship can follow. Leads shift, open and close with the movement of the ice.

Mainmast: The middle and often the largest mast in a ship. In a two-masted vessel, depending on how close the mast is set to the centre, it can be described as either the mainmast or the mizzenmast.

Mizzenmast: The aftermost mast, the mast closest to the stern.

Poop deck: The area of deck at the stern, usually describing a small deck built over the weather, or main deck.

Port: Left.

Rigging: The various lines that support the masts, handle sails and move the cargo. Standing rigging supports the masts and is usually tarred hemp or steel wire; running rigging is untarred hemp and is tied off at various places along the deck.

Rubrail: A timber that runs along the side of the ship, just above the waterline, to protect the hull against damage from wharves, pilings and other ships.

Starboard: Right.

Stem: The timber that forms the bow or the front of the ship.

Sternpost: The timber that forms the rear or the tail end of the ship. The rudder is attached to the sternpost.

Windlass: A special type of winch used to raise the ship's anchors. It is located at the forward end of the ship near the bow.

Bibliography

Books

Bassett, John M., *Henry Larsen*. Don Mills, Ontario: Fitzhenry and Whiteside, 1980.

Berton, Pierre, *The Arctic Grail: The Quest for the North West Passage and the North Pole, 1818-1909*. Toronto: McClelland and Stewart, 1988.

Clarke, Tom E., *The Mounties Patrol the Sea*. Philadelphia: The Westminster Press, 1969.

Delgado, James P., *Made for the Ice: A Report on the Wreck of the Hudson's Bay Company Ship* Baymaud, *ex-Polarskibet Maud*. Vancouver: Vancouver Maritime Museum and the Underwater Archaeological Society of British Columbia, 1997.

——, *Across the Top of the World: The Quest for the Northwest Passage*. Vancouver and Toronto: Douglas & McIntyre, 1999.

Farrar, Sgt. F.S., *Arctic Assignment: The Story of the* St. Roch. Toronto: The Macmillan Company of Canada, 1958.

Francis, Daniel, *Discovery of the North: The Exploration of Canada's Arctic*. Edmonton: Hurtig Publishers, 1986.

Larsen, Henry A., *Reports and Other Papers Relating to the Two Voyages of the R.C.M. Police Schooner "St. Roch" Through the North West Passage*. Ottawa: The King's Printer, 1945, reprint edition, Vancouver: Vancouver Maritime Museum, 2000.

——, Frank R. Sheer and Edvard Omholt-Jensen, *The Big Ship*. Toronto: McClelland and Stewart, 1967.

MacInnes, Tom, *Klengenberg of the Arctic*. London and Toronto: Jonathan Cape, 1932.

Morrison, William R., *Showing the Flag: The Mounted Police and Canadian Sovereignty in the North, 1894-1925*. Vancouver: University of British Columbia Press, 1985.

Smith, Lisa, *Travels with* St. Roch: *A Book for Kids*. Vancouver: Time Talk Press, 2001.

Steele, Harwood, *Policing the Arctic: The Story of the Conquest of the Arctic by the Royal Canadian Mounted Police*. London: Jarrolds Publishers, 1936.

Thompson, John Beswarick, *The More Northerly Route*. Ottawa: Parks Canada, 1978.

Tranter, G.J., *Plowing the Arctic: Being an Account of the Voyage of the R.C.M.P. "St. Roch" Through the North West Passage from West to East*. Toronto: Longmans, Green and Co., 1945.

Articles

Delgado, James P., "Arctic Ghost," *Equinox*, May 1997.

Grant, Shelagh, "Why *St. Roch*? Why the Northwest Passage? Why 1940? New Answers to Old Questions," *Arctic*, 46 (1), March 1993.

Johnston, V.K., "Canada's Title to the Arctic Islands," *Canadian Historical Review*, XIX (1), March 1933.

Larsen, Henry A., "The Conquest of the Northwest Passage: The Arctic Voyages of the *St. Roch*, 1940-44," *Geographical Journal* 110 (nos. 1-3), July-September 1947.

Olsen, Joe, "Could the *St. Roch* Survive The North?" *Scarlet and Gold*, 57th Edition, 1975.

Panipakuttuk, Joe, "The Reminiscences of Joe Panipakuttuk," *north*, XVI (2), January-February 1969.

Robinson, J. Lewis, "Conquest of the Northwest Passage by R.C.M.P. Schooner *St. Roch*," *The Canadian Geographical Journal*, February 1945.

White, Bill, and Howard White, "Sailing on the *St. Roch*," in Howard White, ed., *Raincoast Chronicles Sixteen*. Madeira Park, B.C.: Harbour Publishing, 1983.

Manuscripts

W.B. and M.H. Chung Library, Vancouver Maritime Museum.

Burrard Dry Dock Co., Ltd., Original builder's plans, Hull Number 114 (1928).

Foster, Myles F., "Reminiscences."

Larsen, Henry, private journal, 1928-1934, 1944.

Oliver, Nancy, ed., "Orientation Guide and Training Manual."

St. Roch ephemeral files.

Thompson, John Beswarick, "The Arctic and *St. Roch*" (1973).

Index

Alcan 31, 51
Alexander, HMS 4
Amundsen, Roald 7, 14, 28, 31
Anderton, Andy 19
Andreasson, Ole 40
Aqiguq 26
Arctic (steamship) 11

Back, George 5
Baffin, William 3
Baymaud (schooner) see *Maud*
Beechey, William F. 4
Bernier, Joseph Elzear 11
Blossom, HMS 4
Burrard Dry Dock Company 12, 13, 15, 24, 53
Burrard Iron Works 55
Burton, Ken 48, 49, 50
Bylot, Robert 3

Canadian Polar Expedition 11
Cashin, Billy 43
Caulkin, Thomas B. 13, 28, 31
Chartrand, Albert 21, 34-35, 49
Columbus, Christopher 1
Cook, James 3

Davis, John 3
Dease, Peter 5
Discovery (barque) 3
Dymond, Carolyn 48

Equalla 34
Erebus, HMS 5, 6

Farrar, Fred 21
Fort James (HBC Supply Ship) 24
Foster, Jack 16, 17, 18, 56
Fram (Polar Expedition Ship) 14

Franklin, John 4, 5-6, 33, 41, 49
Franklin, Lady Jane 6
Frederick, John 48
Frobisher, Martin 1-2
Fury, HMS 5

Gillen, William Hugh 15, 16, 17, 19, 20, 23
Gjøa (sloop) 7, 8, 31
Griper, HMS 4

Hadley, Dean 50
Hall, Ken 44
Halliday, Tom 13, 14, 54
Hartung, Mike 50
Hearne, Samuel 4
Hecla, HMS 4, 5
Henri, Father Gustav 34
Hudson's Bay Company 3, 5, 6, 14, 35
Hudson, Henry 3
Hunt, Pat 34, 40

Isabella, HMS 4

Johnson, Rudolph 40, 45, 48

Kamookak, Louie 49
Kells, Robert 20
Kelly, Pat 19
Kembel, Roger 50
Klengenberg, Christian 30

Labrador (icebreaker) 45
Lapointe, Ernest 13
Larsen, Beverly 29, 50
Larsen, Doreen Riedel 29, 50, 51
Larsen, Gordon 29, 50
Larsen, Henry Asbjorn 13, 15, 16, 18, 19, 20, 22, 23, 24, 26, 28-29, 30-35, 36, 37, 38, 39-44, 45, 48, 49, 50, 54, 55, 56, 57, 58
Larsen, Mary Hargreaves 29

M'Clintock, Francis Leopold 6
MacBrien, Sir James 30
MacKenzie, Alexander 4
Maid of Orleans (schooner) 28, 29
Matonabbe 4
May, John 50
Mellis, Robert 48, 49
Maud (Polar Exploration Ship) 13, 14
Millennium Bureau of Canada 51
Moodie, J.D. 11
Moscrop, Arthur 13
Morrison, William 12
Mowat, Farley 8

Newson, Gladys 15
North West Mounted Police 9

Olsen, Joe 16, 18, 23, 48
Omdahl, Oscar 28
Operation Muskox 43

Pallaq, Anne 41
Panipaqkuttuk, Joe and family 40-41, 42, 43, 49
Panipaqkuttuk, Mary 41
Parks Canada 46, 47
Parry, Hugh 50
Parry, W.J. "Dad" 50
Parry, William Edward 4, 5
Parsloe, Terry 18, 20
Peters, G.W. "Bill" 32, 40, 48
Pumps and Power Ltd. 56

Labrador Rae, John 5, 6
Ross, John 4, 5
Royal Vancouver Yacht Club 45
Russill, Lloyd 40

St. Roch Preservation Campaign 47
St. Roch II Voyage of Rediscovery 47-51
Simon Fraser (icebreaker) 48, 49

Simpson, Thomas 5
Terminal City Ironworks 56
Terror, HMS 5, 6
Theodore Roosevelt (steamship) 28
Tomsett, Art 50
Totalik, Adam 49
TrendWest Resorts 51

Unalga (Coast Guard cutter) 18
Union Diesel Company 19, 55

Vancouver, City of 45, 46, 47
Vancouver Foundation 48
Vancouver, George 3
Vancouver Maritime Museum 46, 47, 51
Vancouver School Board 48
Victory (steamship) 5
Village Belle (schooner) 11
Viguq, Soopi 41

White, Bill 25, 36, 37
Wood, Stuart Taylor 12, 13, 31, 32, 39